Changing Faces

The Secret to Ethically Growing an Aesthetics Business

Richard Crawford-Small

WWW.GET-KNOWN.CO.UK

*For everyone out there trying to make
a difference, I salute you.*

*And to the long-suffering Crawford-Small family,
Amy, Lana, Isaac, Toby & Persephone.*

To "The Club"

Thank you for your love, trust and faith xx

TESTIMONIALS

"I started my business 12 months before I met Richard, and my turnover was around about £12,000. Even through lockdown, I managed to grow my business. And my turnover has now tripled. I've changed from looking sideways at competitors, to staying in my own lane and focusing on me and my business. Aesthetic Entrepreneurs has given me the confidence to grow my business. As a nurse, it's very hard to get out of the nursing mindset and get focused; Richard has just helped me develop my business attitude and given me the confidence to grow. I would say the main thing with having Aesthetic Entrepreneurs involved in my business is that I tend to work smarter, not harder – I put my prices up, I've learned to know my worth and invest in myself, not just buy new shiny equipment, and that's really helped my business grow as I was like a magpie, and I've learnt I've got everything in place to grow already.

"People think, 'Oh, what, you're paying for a business coach?', but actually Richard pays for himself. He makes you more accountable, and I love being involved in the Aesthetic Entrepreneurs programme and having all the information to hand on the MAETRIX to help you grow.

"One of the main things that I have taken from being part of Aesthetic Entrepreneurs is that I'm no longer feeling isolated in the field of aesthetics. I've met like-minded people. We can talk protocols together, we bounce ideas off each other and, yeah, I just feel like I'm no longer isolated. I've got a nice group of people that I can work alongside."

**MICHELLE WORTHINGTON,
MICHELLE WORTHINGTON AESTHETIC HEALTH**

"Before I came across Aesthetic Entrepreneurs and Richard, I was building business myself with very little background knowledge, very little support. I'd had various business coaches before, but I'd got to a point where I was 10 days from going out of business. I was following Aesthetic Entrepreneurs on Facebook, and Richard had put a post out about something, and I can't even remember what it was now, and I just answered this post with an emoji, and again, I can't remember which one, and Richard spotted me and dragged me kicking and screaming into Aesthetic Entrepreneurs.

"And from that day, just before Christmas, a few years ago, I then went on to have the biggest turnover in one month that I'd ever had, from being 10 days from going out of business. So without Aesthetic Entrepreneurs and without Richard, I wouldn't have a business. And since then things have progressed. I've made lots of changes to the business, paired it right back. And I'm at a position now, where we're about to do a bit of a relaunch, bit of a sort of new direction, new focus, and it feels very different to how it did those years ago, before I came across Aesthetic Entrepreneurs."

SALLY WAGSTAFF, SALLY WAGSTAFF AESTHETIC

CONTENTS

Who is this book for?   9

What will you get from this book?   15

Who is Richard Crawford-Small?   21

Getting started   27

How big is that robot?   33

The world reimagined   39

The rise of the Aesthetic Entrepreneur   45

Being the best   57

"Know thyself"   63

Goal setting   73

My journey   87

The six key mistakes   95

MISTAKE NUMBER 1 – Not being authentic   101

MISTAKE NUMBER 2 – Telling the wrong stories   107

MISTAKE NUMBER 3 – Not enough understanding   115

MISTAKE NUMBER 4 – Not creating an experience   121

MISTAKE NUMBER 5 – Trying to skip the struggle   129

MISTAKE NUMBER 6 – Starting too big   135

Take responsibility   143

The three home truths   151

The journey to success   159

Creating new offerings   201

The sales Jedi   211

Final thoughts and next steps   219

"Who am I?"

DEREK ZOOLANDER – ZOOLANDER (2013)

WHO IS THIS BOOK FOR?

I originally wrote this book in 2016 with the vision of helping Medical Aesthetic businesses learn how to grow a business, to show that it is possible to combine a commercial objective with medical ethics, and that is still important. However, little did I know that this book would actually become my own guide and bible as I rebuilt my business in 2018 following the collapse of my software business. During that time, and in the years since then, I've actually realised that is really not who this book is for, so I've come back from the future to do a Star Wars Special Edition on it. Han shot first by the way.

In these pages is the knowledge and wisdom that enabled me to pivot from being a software company to founding the Aesthetic

Entrepreneurs, and during that process I went on a bit of a journey, with an amazing lady called Kelly.

Most people who will read this book are stressed, working far too hard, not looking after themselves. You might have just finished your training, and you're probably sitting there thinking, "right... now what? How do I get clients? How do I get more clients? What the f**k is this business thing actually all about?"

You may be in a dazed whirlwind. You may have tried a few things which have not really worked (booooo) and tried a few other things which have worked (yaaaay). I want you to start at that point, I want you to start at the realisation that that is what you are; so congratulations, well done, you've taken an amazing step forward, but you're now in the big, scary world.

There are a few rules to being an entrepreneur.

The main rule is that you are going to be shitting yourself pretty much every day for the next five years. You're going to have successes, you're going to have failures, and you're going to go through this experience three times every day. This is not a ride for the faint hearted. I'm not saying this to be scary, I'm not saying this to terrify or put you off – I just believe that a healthy dose of reality is what's needed. Shitting yourself, I think, is a very natural part of life and business. It's the start of the process of gaining clarity and the real start of the entrepreneurial journey. Waking up in the middle of the night, feeling a bit sick and not knowing how you will pay the mortgage, is a feeling that we will all share at some point.

This is not for everyone. It will be hard.

"The mistake wasn't doing it; the mistake was putting everything I had into it."

I was told in a meeting that I do things very differently to a lot of other "aesthetic business coaches", in that we at Aesthetic Entrepreneurs don't do cookie cutter courses or workshops that just give you a few PDFs and a video. I'd not really thought that much about what other people do, as I tend to just focus on our own community and clients. It got me thinking about why I do what I do. One of the key things for me is that I have failed, badly and often, and I don't shy away from that fact. Instead, the failures drive me and teach me how not to do something. I also learn a huge amount personally from them, and I want to share this, not to stop people making mistakes, but to guide them through the process of building something.

My software was, on the face of it, a massive failure, and I put everything I had into it. The mistake wasn't doing it; the mistake was putting everything I had into it. The level of risk was too high, but I was way too emotionally involved to see it objectively. The market changed direction, investors got cold feet, and boom – shut down. I had no real income and no plan. I spent the next 12 weeks head down, grafting, working with the founding members of Aesthetic Entrepreneurs to build that but also rebuild myself.

It reminded me that to grow I needed to exercise three things every day.

 Focus

 Consistency

 Discipline

This is where it starts and ends, and this created the Aesthetic Entrepreneurs.

So was it really a complete failure?

Being open and honest about the times I really ballsed things up is just something I will always do. But also being open and honest about what it actually takes to build a business is also something I will always do too. No sugar coating, just effective support, high-quality thinking and a positive attitude.

So, who is Kelly?

"Hi, I'm Kelly, I started my aesthetic business in 2016. I went to Harley Street and did the courses, I was a senior nurse in the NHS, a leader, a manager, I had a website, I opened the doors and... nothing, no clients! What was I doing wrong?" K

"Why don't you knock it off with them nega-tive waves? Why don't you dig how beautiful it is out here? Why don't you say something righteous and hopeful for a change?"

ODDBALL – KELLY'S HEROES (1970)

WHAT WILL YOU GET FROM THIS BOOK?

This book will get you started on the path to understanding your value and creating an ethical and successful aesthetic business. I will show you how to move through the boutique wilderness on your way to the Valhalla of Lifestyle. From there you can move to a Performance business generating quite quickly with the right foundations in place, the foundations you'll get from this book.

You will learn how to:

- Simplify and reduce that sense of overwhelm

- Build a digital business in an analogue industry

- Structure your business to provide experiences, not just treatments

- Attract the right clients who respect you and will pay

- Avoid some of the major pitfalls new business owners fall into

- Create marketing assets that really work

- Create focus, consistency and discipline

- Save your time, and money

- Align your business with your personal goals

- Create a sense of purpose beyond just making money

- Build a business you are proud of, not a hobby that drains you

- Become an unstoppable Aesthetic Entrepreneur.

It will also give you some tips and quick wins, and lessons from some others who have walked the path that you are about to take.

People like Sally, Kelly, Michelle and Stevie.

During my nearly 20 years in Medical Aesthetics, many clients have typically said that they have challenges in standing out from the competition, driving growth and additional profit, and this has always come down to one major issue.

Aesthetic business don't know their value, so they price low, use offers to grow the business and attract the wrong clients. Many are frustrated and don't really know how to create social media content, how to set pricing, get the right clients, manage time, create process, build a service suite. If you have never been shown or taught how to, why would you know?

Spending thousands of pounds on clinical skills is a waste unless you invest in the knowledge, tools and talent to commercialise those skills.

This was EXACTLY what my client Kelly was doing when I met her. Kelly was a classic boutique aesthetic business, a nurse out of the NHS who has a couch, a wall of certificates, a few friends/clients, and was working out of her daughter's bedroom. I met Kelly, as a favour to a friend at the rugby club. As she was local, I popped in to see her and we had a chat. She was absolutely lovely but had no real idea on how to move forward. She was getting lots of conflicting advice, so I gave Kelly a copy of *Changing Faces*, a few tips on how to get off and running, and off I went.

A few weeks later I got a message: "It only went and bloody worked!". In all honesty, I can't remember at all what it was that I did or said that worked, but Kelly got a win, and that was all she needed.

Tail in the air, she's been unstoppable ever since, and only a few years later, Kelly has her own clinic space, which she opened during the 2020 lockdown, a thriving business with its own identity, and I'm very proud of her and pleased to have helped Florence get her bedroom back.

"I was introduced to RCS and he gave me what I needed, the confidence to believe I could do this and the tools to do it. I'm good with instructions and I knew I needed to take advice from someone who knew more about this than I did. I could see how much he was living through this process himself. It was reassuring to see his journey, knowing he had years of experience within the aesthetics business. It didn't feel like jargon-heavy slides and buzzwords but knowledge and skills from personal experience, old and new." K

I meet many, many people like Kelly and not all succeed. They can't get out of their own way, they can't stop the fear from crippling them, they can't shake off the nurse and release the entrepreneur. Kelly succeeded because she has implemented, she takes action, does the "thing" and learns. She LOVES being an Aesthetic Entrepreneur, and in my time-travel rewrite, the 2016 vintage Kelly is the person I'm writing this book for. If I could have handed Kelly a better version of Changing Faces, what would be in it?

Well, imagine if she had a message from herself five years later telling her that everything would be OK, what would the 2021 Aesthetic Entrepreneurs say to themselves in 2016?

"I'd tell myself to believe in my skill, trust the process, nothing happens overnight, don't believe the hype, surround yourself with like-minded souls and get a coach"

"Warn that test lab in Wuhan they need better security"

"Buy Bitcoin"

"Get a coach"

We can't go back in time, all we can do is go forward – so what are you going to create from here?

Let's get to work.

"We wanna be free! We wanna be free to do what we wanna do. We wanna be free to ride. We wanna be free to ride our machines without being hassled by The Man! ... And we wanna get loaded."

HEAVENLY BLUE – THE WILD ANGELS (1966)

WHO IS RICHARD CRAWFORD-SMALL?

'm an award-winning entrepreneur specialising in creating beautiful aesthetic businesses by inspiring the people behind them.

I've been in the aesthetics sector for over 15 years and have developed unique and proven methodologies that will grow your business by starting better conversations with the right client, building relationships and converting those relationships to sales.

I've worked with hundreds of businesses globally, from small independent clinics right through to multi-million-dollar chains, to help them maximise the lifetime value of their patients and deliver a consistent, compliant and comprehensive service every time.

I'm also the founder of the Aesthetic Entrepreneurs group, the fastest growing aesthetic business community online, and the author of the bestselling book *Changing Faces* – the secret of creating a beautiful aesthetic business.

Look forward to getting to know you guys and to help you achieve what you need!

I am also...

A bum, who likes nothing better than sitting in front of the TV watching rugby, films or *Fast N' Loud* on Discovery Channel.

A husband, to my talented wife Amy who is a fashion designer, entrepreneur and creator of Do The Twist headscarves (www.dothetwist.co.uk), and dad to four rampaging children.

Ex-military, having served in the Royal Navy for eight years, I represented Royal Navy and a host of other teams at rugby union, had many injuries, jacked it in and now do karate instead. Less painful, believe it or not.

A lover of Harley-Davidson motorcycles (I have a few) and the freedom and headspace that motorcycling provides. I ride all year round as well. Here are my social media channels, feel free to drop me a line!

www.themaetrix.com/member/49/Richard_Crawford-Small

www.facebook.com/groups/theaestheticentrepreneurs

www.aestheticentrepreneurs.com

www.facebook.com/RCrawfordSmall

www.instagram.com/rcs_insta

https://podcasts.apple.com/gb/podcast/aesthetic-entrepreneur/id1495236365

https://open.spotify.com/show/5sU6sm3xgjoZhVZL1mzU62?si=4r-YEa_06Tg-RrxWkHJaDeg

PART 1

WHERE ARE WE AND HOW DID WE GET HERE?

"Human beings, who are almost unique in having the ability to learn from the experience of others, are also remarkable for their apparent disinclination to do so."

**DOUGLAS ADAMS –
THE HITCHHIKER'S GUIDE TO THE GALAXY (1978)**

GETTING STARTED

One of the most challenging but rewarding consultancy projects I undertake is working with growing aesthetic businesses who are struggling to really get things going. It's challenging for a number of reasons, but the primary one is a lack of resources. Now, resources for me are simply time, energy and money. While it's great to have all three in abundance, the vast majority of Medical Aesthetic start-ups are operated by single owners looking for additional income or to move their careers in a different direction. This lack of resources is compounded by the fact that most suppliers are not geared up to support new businesses. As with all start-ups, the big questions are, "How do I start?" and "Will it work?"

While I can't guarantee that your business will succeed, I can provide you with a starting point and a solid platform to improve the chances of success greatly.

From here you can work with this book in three different ways:

1. You can scan read it and consider it a box ticked.

2. You can read it and mark chapters to come back to and reread.

3. You can treat it as a training programme.

I recommend option 3, it's the one that will give you the most value and impact. You have to remember I've LIVED this book, and it's been cunningly designed to rebuild your business in the next few months. So please, work with me, through this book, as a partner. It's not just a series of exercises and nice ideas, but the actual process I went through, and I'm still going through every day to build my business.

To help you do this you can find lots of information and support in the Aesthetic Entrepreneurs MAETRIX system at **www.themae-trix.com**. The MAETRIX is the second brain of the AE. Designed to have everything that an Aesthetic Entrepreneur needs to grow and develop in one place, the MAETRIX is the one-stop shop for high-quality education, insight, coaching and inspiration to enable our clients to realise their full potential. It's a platform like no other, that combines learning management, community and content to provide a unique and highly effective environment for learning and skills development. MAETRIX stands for "Multifunctional Aesthetic Entrepreneurs TRaining and Information eXchange, and was named by one of our clients, Dr Louise Hallam.

Scan this QR code to get access to the free resources!

Once you have registered, you'll get an email with a link to complete "Your Business Growth Scorecard". To know how successful you have been, you first need to understand how unsuccessful you have been, and this scorecard covers the main points any start-up business needs to measure themselves against, and at the end you will have an accurate picture of where you are. My clients and I complete this weekly in the early stages of our consultancy, and monthly after that, and it is always with a great sense of pride that we see significant increase in the scorecard percentages and watch it correlate with increases in profit. I want you to take a couple of minutes here and complete your scorecard.

Once you've completed it, you'll get a FREE Business Playbook and access to resources that will give you tips and insight on how to improve your skills in Entrepreneurship, Planning, Culture, Business Efficiency, Sales, Getting Clients, Time Management, and more.

Read each question below, and give yourself one point for a yes, and zero for a no. No fudging; be brutally honest with yourself. "Maybe", "I'm not sure" and "I think so" are all zero scores.

1. Do you often feel overwhelmed?

2. Do you feel comfortable with selling?

3. Do you have a clear vision, mission and values for your business?

4. Have you got a business plan you can share right now?

5. Are you clear on what makes your business special or unique?

6. Do you feel frustrated that your marketing doesn't seem to perform?

7. Do you feel like your business is always competing on price?

8. Do you know your ideal customer avatar?

9. On a scale of 1-100%, how happy are you with the growth and development of your business in the last three years?

10. Do you have a designed and automated client journey?

11. Are you GENUINELY excited about the idea of rebuilding and scaling?

12. What percentage of your revenue is generated by ongoing treatment plans?

13. What is your current annual business turnover? (This doesn't count toward the score – just for reference.)

Now you have your benchmark score, your goal is to improve on this score, as improvements on the score are improvements in your business. I'll let you into a little secret – I use scorecards on my own business, and it is very difficult to score top marks. I designed it and have NEVER scored top marks on my own test. The shame! However, what resulted was a complete reworking of my business model from the bottom up – new products, new processes, new partnerships and a new mantra. "Get the right people in the right place, doing the right things, and you get the right result."

Now, I don't like being told what to do, and I have a deep-rooted sense of rebellion that finds the very existence of a plan distasteful. This is not my finest trait. If you are like me, I can sympathise as you will find this next exercise a real struggle, but don't worry. If you're a creative, your time will come.

Creating a plan and executing it requires focus, consistency and discipline. But the harsh reality is that you need a business plan; you cannot run headlong into something and see all of the angles, pitfalls, opportunities and upsides. Business plans give you insight to help you see these issues, not to control and stifle your creativity.

That said, I really struggled until I designed our O.R.B.I.T Product Development Model. Once I had this in place, planning became a much more entertaining process, but don't worry about that now, we will cover the O.R.B.I.T Model in more detail in the chapter entitled "Creating New Offerings".

"I'll be back."

THE TERMINATOR — THE TERMINATOR (1984)

HOW BIG
IS THAT ROBOT?

I magine you could go back in time to 2016 and have a conversation with your clients. What would you say to them? How would you even begin to articulate the events of the past few years? I wouldn't even sound plausible.

"There is a nuclear war and a huge robot from the future that looks like a bodybuilder is trying to kill you."

Yeah right!

"A global pandemic called COVID-19 is going to shut down the entire economy and thousands of people will die from it."

How big is that robot?

Bloody huge, and I've travelled back through time to help you to benefit from the lessons that we have just learned, and there are some huge ones. Yet, without this book, I probably would not have had a business anyway. Around 2018, I took a good old-fashioned business kicking and nearly lost everything. I used this book as my own bible. I had to think about how we were going to redevelop the business. The key was to have multiple streams, digital assets, products, diversification and solve big problems. What happened next is frankly all a bit of a blur. The summer holidays basically consisted of me at my MacBook for hours on end trying to build something from nothing. I didn't realise what it was that I was building but I knew I wanted to get back into pure marketing. I knew I had a good process, I had a solid understanding of it, but I had to apply my own logic to it.

With guidance, support, being told to "reverse engineer this", "look at things from the clients' point of view", "have you thought that through?" we began to piece together the semblance of a plan.

This is not something I did on my own, but we gradually rebuilt our services using the methodology, the models and lessons from my book, *Changing Faces*. At the end of the day, there are some ways to speed up the process if you already have a reputation, experience, a few products and a contact list to die for. I had the reputation, the contacts and the experience, but I had no products or services to offer them.

The fundamental goal of any business is to solve a problem. The real trick is to find out what that problem is, but unfortunately everyone will lie to you. Cold leads, warm leads, hot leads, conversations, relationships and sales are all totally irrelevant if you have not identified the problem, found enough people with that problem, built the relationships to get your clients to trust you to solve that problem, and then actually be able to solve it. If the problem's big enough, then so is the amount of money.

Fortunately for me, the problems were exactly the same as they had always been, but the difference was the solution I created to solve them wasn't anywhere near ready, so I needed a different one. I needed to create a tribe, a community that supported each other and shared my values.

This is where the idea to create the Aesthetic Entrepreneurs came from. I've created Facebook groups before and they didn't work, and the reason they didn't work is because I created them with the aim to sell to people. I created it with the aim to commercialise it immediately.

This was the conversation:

GOOD MORNING.

MORNING.

JOIN MY GROUP.

WHY?

SO I CAN SELL MY STUFF TO YOU.

NO, GET STUFFED.

OK.

Clearly, this is totally the wrong way to approach all of this, and actually it's the approach to sales many take but should actually avoid at all costs. You need to build the group and the community, establish your credibility, your authority and build trust. When, and only when, you have built trust will people work with you as a client; which is true for me and it's true for you here, reading this book.

If you take one thing away from this book, it's that. Stop selling and build the relationship. Stop thinking about social media as something that is NOT human to human – it totally is. It baffles me how people can behave appallingly when behind a keyboard, yet nice as pie to your face. Just because you are nice when we meet, I still think you're a twat. And so does everyone else.

You must not forget that you are speaking to a human, a person, with likes and dislikes, the same as you. If you meet a nice guy/girl and go out on a date, will you try and jump into bed with him/her on the first night? If that's your goal, then best of luck, and sometimes you'll be successful and sometimes you won't.

But is this really who you are?

Is this one to take home to Mum?

You need to build a relationship which requires an investment from both you and your date or, back to business terms, your potential client. You have to do things to make sure that you understand and appreciate that relationship you are building is the right relationship to build.

Create huge amounts of added value to the client journey, and make sure that your clients return every time and generate revenue by increasing your clients' satisfaction levels.

By understanding how harnessing the principles of experience economies, you can transform your processes into a revenue generating powerhouse, by creating a memorable step by step and enriched client journey that adds massive value to the experience.

That is what *Changing Faces* taught me, and it was an incredible lesson, but it's not the only lesson I've come back to teach you.

"I learnt quickly I couldn't be all things to all people so started speaking to my community. Solving their problems, not just telling them about treatments. I was taught to sell to give value to my clients and learnt that it wasn't a four-letter word. I learnt my value, no more offers, no more competitions."

"I am putting myself to the fullest possible use, which is all I think that any conscious entity can ever hope to do."

HAL 9000 – 2001: A SPACE ODYSSEY (1968)

THE WORLD REIMAGINED

Since I first put pen to paper in 2016 and wrote this book, the world as we know it has changed on a global scale, and I couldn't go ahead and publish it without acknowledging that and adding in an additional chapter that addressed it. On March 16 2020, the coronavirus hit the markets. It had been around since the end of December 2019, maybe even before, but it hit the markets in March.

Just like 65 million years ago when a meteor hit the earth and wiped out the dinosaurs, coronavirus created an extinction environment in which some types of business wouldn't survive. It caused a seismic shift – a massive societal change. One word that was bandied around was "unprecedented", and I can't actually think of a better word than that. There's a wonderful quote from Vladimir Ilyich Lenin that says, "*There are decades where nothing happens, and weeks where decades happen*".

The weeks between mid-March 2020 until early June 2020 were those weeks. The COVID-19 pandemic forced many of us to make changes to the way we run our businesses, and we still don't fully know what the long-term impact will be. However, as an entrepreneur you will always come up against challenges – the trick is to start seeing them as opportunities for growth and grabbing them by the balls with both hands.

The coronavirus pandemic threw us all into a new economy – an experience economy underpinned by digital technologies. Retail was pushed five years into the future in terms of the demand placed on it from an economic and digital point of view, and that meant not a single part of society wasn't touched by it. The online economy is not just here, but it's here to stay. Commentators are saying that businesses won't be back to "normal" for some time. I would say some time means never. There is no "back to normal" there's only the "new normal" – it may be a tagline, but it's true.

As business owners and entrepreneurs, we have to evolve, you need to be a digital business in an analogue industry. If you do this, you will have a competitive advantage so huge it will be like bringing a rocket to a bicycle race.

To do that we need to look at the opportunities, what we can achieve, where we can focus and what we can and can't control. What we can control is what we do as individuals or as business owners – the decisions that we make. What we can't control is what's going to happen in the market. If the last few years has shown us anything it's that you can't really control what happens in the world.

I'm often talking about value but it's even more important now than ever. Things have turned on their head and who has the highest value in society has changed. Cristiano Ronaldo, one of the highest paid athletes in the world, was unemployed, had zero worth and was of no use whatsoever.

However, people who were traditionally the lowest paid or lowest valued jobs in society such as cleaners and delivery drivers were becoming more highly valued. But where does aesthetics fit into this?

There was a significant change in the market dynamic, and it happened overnight.

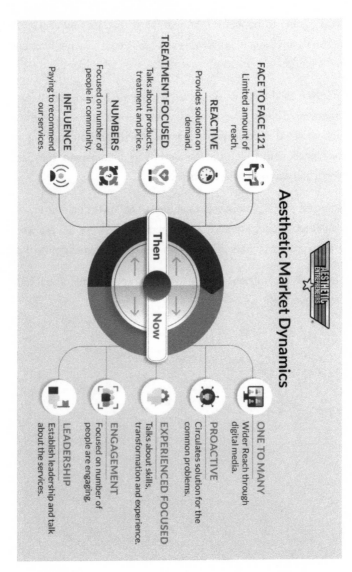

Figure 1: How the Pandemic changed the Aesthetic Market

At the beginning of March 2020, you made your money one-to-one, face-to-face. That was how you got paid – providing treatments for a person and being in the company of that person. You were genuinely quite reactive, and you could afford to be quite reactive. People would walk in and tell you what they wanted.

You were treatment-focused, so a lot of your attention was drawn towards what treatments you provided and what products you used. From a marketing point of view, your social media could, to put it bluntly, be pretty vanilla, and you'd get away with it. You looked at the numbers a lot – how many likes you had, how many followers you had – what we call "vanity metrics". And it was all influencer led. Who was doing what, where and when and with who, was driving the decision making process in society and in marketing.

Fast forward a few weeks and all of a sudden no one was making any money treating people face-to-face as individuals. Everyone was forced to look at online models. It became about engagement, not numbers. It was noisy with a lot of people competing for air-time and digital space. Influencers became irrelevant – they were all sat at home doing selfies in front of the garages.

So, in order to be heard above the noise, I guided my clients to start focusing on experience rather than treatments – vision and values kind of stuff, how they achieve certain things for certain people – and, for me, this strategy stands whether we are in lockdown or not. It's all about value. When you value a business, that valuation is usually based on profit times a multiple. There are lots of things that can negatively affect that value, for example, high costs, no recurring revenue and debt.

There are also things that affect it positively such as culture, vision, values, leadership, personal brand, creating an online business and product innovation.

All those things have a positive impact in the valuation of your business.

V=P/E - Value = Price over Experience

This is not wishy-washy, airy-fairy stuff, this is real business logic that if applied will increase the value of your business. Value is also important when it comes to your clients. They will calculate this by measuring the price over experience – how much they paid over the experience they had. If your experience is not up to scratch, then your price will have to come down because the value isn't there. Think about this as an equation, people are making this calculation in their heads over and over again without knowing it: "Is the price I'm paying worth what I'm getting?" If you are not talking about the experience they will have, essentially all you're doing is talking about price, but you need to trade in the Experience Economy, and we have a blueprint to help you do it.

This is what underpins our Business programmes.

But we'll explore all of that later.

"I always wanted my own space. I didn't think it would ever happen, but in my coaching with Richard, he assured me that he knew it would. Not only did it happen, it happened during a pandemic." K

"I love lamp."

BRICK TAMLAND — ANCHORMAN (2004)

THE RISE OF THE AESTHETIC ENTREPRENEUR

One thing I will always be incredibly proud of is how we all pulled together to reflect, relearn, regroup, refocus, and rebuild ourselves and the business. At one point in this story, we had four months where we needed to get our income moving again before we ran out of money, and I used the knowledge and insight in this book to do it.

This chapter is about how it happened, as best I can remember.

The first thing that you need to do if you are going to rebuild something is relearn. I had to turn my hand to something very, very quickly, and there's a wonderful saying attributed to Albert Einstein, which is that *"We cannot solve our problems with the same thinking we used when we created them. We must learn to see the world anew"*.

We have to change our perspective and allow ourselves to get a new view on what the problem is and really accept the failure to understand what went wrong, and I went super deep into this during the year. The type of project ideas that I tend to have are always incredibly ambitious and generally a bit "out there", but I can't help it, it's in my DNA to innovate.

When I think about my history, there was one huge lesson that I had not learnt, and it was the fundamental reason behind why I'd narrowly missed the target, and it's also the NUMBER ONE reason why a lot of aesthetic clinics also fail. The key lesson I had not fully appreciated or understood was that I had not spent enough time or energy developing a deep understanding of the problems that my clients had. I thought I knew, and I believed that I knew, but **knowing is much better than believing**, so I knew I needed to go back to basics and get a PhD level education in the problems that affected the market. For years I'd been in this bubble of hubris and foolishly felt that if I had asked my clients what their problems were, I'd expose myself as a charlatan who didn't know what he was doing. Nothing could be further from the truth, and "I don't know" is a perfectly acceptable answer to a question that you don't actually know the answer to.

Watching someone trying to conjure up and make something up on the spot is something I find quite funny now, and if I don't know, rather than trying to invent the answer or solution without any insight, I'll often now just ask this question back. The challenges you have at the start of your career are not ones that you have in the middle and they're certainly the ones that you have at the end and taking the time to research that gave me massive insight and understanding. When I'm talking to clients now, I understand WHY you want to know certain things and the real importance of that to you. I am totally clued up on what's going on and by taking the time to engage with clients and understand the REAL challenges that you have, I realised that I actually didn't have the right solutions.

Back in 2016, my business model was all over the place, totally unbalanced and didn't play to my core strengths. That was the first big thing I had to change; software is great, but my key skillset is all about coaching. I get a real buzz out of helping people achieve their goals and it's my personal mission. I do love business development, I'm a very accomplished salesperson, and I have an ability to think tactically and strategically at the same time. Yet I'd also developed a skill over the years that had just snuck up on me, entrepreneurship. I think we are often far too afraid to take four, five, six, seven, maybe ten steps back to get our shit together and go again. I had absolutely no choice, because what I was doing wasn't working, but after I did and gained that clarity, the solution became obvious. Reflect in order to relearn and understand what you don't know.

ONCE YOU HAVE THE CLARITY IT'S TIME TO REFOCUS

It's always been in my nature to be a bit of a magpie. I have a tendency to lock onto an idea, work damn hard, become really skilled and develop a great insight, and then, at the perfect time it's about to pay off, get bored, ditch it and go and do something else. While this is great for fun and wondrous variety in a career, it's pretty rubbish if you are trying to actually build something meaningful.

"The chances are that what actually lights you up is the thing that you are really, really good at."

People say play to your strengths, and that is what you have to do. Play to your strengths, minimise your weaknesses, and what I have realised is that once I have learnt how to do something, I need to be able to pass it on to someone else to run with if I run out of enthusiasm.

Most of the time, I tend to get bored with things that are, frankly, boring and I'm a firm believer that you need to get the right people in the right place, doing the right things and you'll get the right result. Accounting and admin bore me rigid, expenses and all that are such a drain. I hated doing them so much that when someone said "get someone else to do them" it was like a weight had been lifted. It sounds daft, but sometimes you really can't see the wood for the trees, and it takes someone to point out to you where you are not being efficient. This is the huge benefit of getting coaching: it helps you focus. The chances are that what actually lights you up is the thing that you are really, really good at. I also enjoy being a pioneer and an innovator but doing something for the first time in the world ever is really, really hard, and actually a pretty terrible idea.

I had to go back to my core, which was sales, marketing, business development and coaching. One massive benefit from leading my technology projects was that I was now re-entering the sector with a whole new skillset. I had been seriously tested and every single part of my business ability had been laid bare, the good and the not so good. I'd managed a team with members in the US, Canada, Russia, India and London, I had worked with the number one financial technologies law firm in the world, I had sat opposite Russian gangsters, I'd negotiated my socks off, and I'd taken a Crypto Initial Coin Offering to the starting line and launched it, something that 80% of them failed to do.

This is all a story for another time.

One of the key things that they won't tell you at the door to Entrepreneur School (well, partly because there isn't an Entrepreneur School – unless you count our workshops), but another lesson I want you to take onboard is that whatever you are thinking about launching, it will take twice as long as you think. It's the big lie that is sold to you by the "Hustle hustle" guru crowd, and it just doesn't get spoken about often enough. All things need time to mature, and change needs time to change. It's not realistic to believe that you can just rock up with your business plan, knock up a Facebook page and expect it to just suddenly rocket. The whole unicorn myth that's been built up around American startups and tech startups etc. is just that, a myth.

Very, very few companies achieve unicorn status. In finance, a unicorn is a privately held startup company with a current valuation of US$1 billion or more, like Uber or Facebook, Airbnb and Deliveroo in the UK. Because these companies suddenly arise from nothing to multi-billion-dollar valuations, it becomes what everybody wants but it's almost impossible to achieve and is totally impossible to predict. However, what will never change are the fundamentals of good, solid economics and business practice. The technologies will change and evolve, but if your business plan is solid and well executed and you're bringing in more money than is going out, then you stand a fighting chance of making it.

Good ideas often do need time to take off. **Being an entrepreneur requires instinct, fortitude and the ability to accept that the world does not run on your schedule.** Sometimes you just have to believe.

There is one thing to remember, and this should give you comfort, there is a pattern to success, and it repeats all the time, everywhere.

"The hardest part about becoming an overnight success is the first 10 years." RCS

Don't believe me?

Check out the quotes at the bottom of the page.

Over the last 12 months, we've been on an incredible journey with Aesthetic Entrepreneurs and recently have formed some incredible partnerships that will accelerate our growth and take AE to the next level. We'll seen as an overnight success by a large part of the aesthetic sector, but in reality the seeds were sown 10 years ago when I took the step and left Allergan.

"You can't reap what you don't sow." ("Let It Grow" – *Illumination Entertainment, The Lorax* 😊)

10 years of mistakes, 10 years of listening to podcasts, 10 years of reading books, 6 years of doing it myself because I know better, 4 years of learning from others who know more than me, 10 years of getting a bit ahead and then screwing it all up, 5 years of building software systems, 20 years of building relationships, 10 years of thinking I've finally cracked it and then realising that you never actually do, 8 years of worrying too much about what other people think, 2 years of then telling the people who you worried about what they thought to sod off, 1 year of really connecting with a core team of A-Players, 10 years of working hard to understand what your clients' problems are, 10 years of working hard to understand what your clients' goals are, 2 years of working hard

to create a solution for them, 2 years of trying to tell them that it works, it really really works, 10 years of getting fat, 10 years of getting fit.

10 years to learn that there is a pattern to success, and it repeats.

Sound familiar?

It should do, and if it doesn't it's probably because you're not far enough down the road. The roadmap for pretty much all businesses is the same, and I've adapted a well-known model for the aesthetic market.

It typically takes:

- Start-up – £0-25K revenue (12-18 months)

- Boutique – £25-£100K (18-60 months)

- Lifestyle – £100-250K (60-80 months)

- Performance – £250-£1M (80-120 months)

- High-Performance – £1-£5M (Up to you)

- Corporate – £5M+ (Probably never)

120 months from Start-up to Performance, and most of your revenue increase will come in the last 20 months.

So, where are you?

Are you ready to dig in for the long haul?

You should be, aesthetics is a VERY resilient and VERY profitable market to be in, if you have the right focus, are consistent with your communication and have the discipline to stay in the game.

The rest is just a matter of trusting the process and allowing time to do the rest of the work.

There is a global change in mindset and business approach going on right now, and it's incredibly exciting. Digital processes and automation are no longer nice to have but MUST haves. **The pandemic was the biggest accelerant to the Experience Economy in history** and proved that businesses with a committed entrepreneur at its core, with a diversified business model, clearly differentiated with above average pricing move through the roadmap faster than those that don't.

It's a golden time in business, and an exhilarating one for me – who wants to be an overnight success in 2031?

Stop trying to see the end of the rainbow, you won't. Stop trying to skip the struggle, you can't.

Set your goal, create your plan, suck it up and get on with it.

You can!

You will!

We're watching you do it!

There are numerous examples of business owners or companies who have launched into diving markets where timing was just not in their favour, or they have just got it wrong.

My project tanked and I had to dig myself right out of it. However, eventually, they made it. That's where the real insights and lessons come from and that is where my new skillset was developed; it was the failure I had experienced that gave me the edge.

Now was the time to build it back up and experience the success.

Lessons from others!

"All overnight success takes about 10 years."

JEFF BEZOS (AMAZON FOUNDER)

"It took about 10 years' time for Shopify to be an overnight success."

TOBIAS LUTKE (SHOPIFY FOUNDER)

"My overnight success was really 15 years in the making. I'd been writing songs since I was 6 and playing in bands and performing since I was 14."

LISA LOEB (SINGER/SONGWRITER)

"When you see someone who has a lot of knowledge, they learned it over time. When you see

someone who has a lot of skills, they developed them over time. When you see someone who has done a lot, they accomplished it over time."

GARY KELLER (KELLER WILLIAMS FOUNDER, AUTHOR OF THE ONE THING)

"The only thing that endures over time is the Law of the Farm. You must prepare the ground, plant the seed, cultivate, and water it if you expect to reap the harvest."

STEPHEN COVEY (THE 7 HABITS OF HIGHLY EFFECTIVE PEOPLE)

"You are the Duke of New York!
You are A Number One."

THE PRESIDENT OF THE UNITED STATES
– ESCAPE FROM NEW YORK (1981)

BEING THE BEST

f I was to ask you if you were the best in the world at what you did, how would you answer? The answer should of course be yes – a beautifully simple and elegant answer to a simple question. The problem is, it's such a simple reply, everyone could answer the question the same way.

Do you know why you are the best at what you do? The answer again should be yes, but this time it's not such a simple answer. The good thing is that everyone could answer this question differently, because everyone has a unique perspective. If you found answering that question difficult, then this book is for you.

UNIQUE SELLING POINTS

Understanding what makes you different from your competition, being able to communicate that difference and why you are the best, is the key to business growth. It's all called your USP (unique selling point). I have another way of describing it – adding a bit of colour.

Now, let me share with you a couple of little secrets: USPs may be unique, but they are rarely original, and USPs are totally made up. Yes, a USP is 100% fabricated. It's been invented to make a product or service appear different from another product or service.

Let me give you an example. Here are four squares.

You are free to take one with you as a gift with my compliments.

Which one would you like, square 1, 2, 3 or 4?

It doesn't matter which one you choose. They are all the same, right?

Well, what if I told you that square 1 isn't actually a square? It's a compact rectangle, while the other three are just boring old squares. You don't want a boring old square, do you?

Awesome Compact Rectangle vs Boring Old Squares.

I'd like to bet that you'd prefer one of those compact rectangles to a boring old square. Why not call all squares compact rectangles from now on?

Of course, we know that the compact rectangle is actually a square, but now it is a square with a USP. I have given you a reason to take it by creating a point of difference and altering your perception of it.

Here's another example.

There are four sales reps sitting in a waiting room, all with an appointment to see a new prospect. They all have identical product offerings and are wearing identical black suits, black shoes and blue shirts.

What is the likelihood of each of them winning the account?

Exactly 25%.

Then one of the reps pulls out his trump card. He goes to the bathroom and changes into a red shirt. What is his likelihood of winning the account now? Is it 25%? Is it 33%? Nope, it's 50%. Because the other three all look the same, he has simply and effectively split the deck, and even though they have exactly the same product, he will have a different conversation with the prospect.

We'll come back to this in a little while. There are examples of USPs in every single purchase we make, from the TVs we watch to the cars we drive, the places we eat to the computers we use.

It's important to remember that buying decisions are all based on emotion then justified with logic, not the other way round. Think about the last major purchase you made. What made you choose that particular product? How does owning it make you feel?

Throughout the years, I've been in hundreds of clinics and seen hundreds of consultations, and I've often felt that with a few small changes, the consultation process in most clinics could be carried out more effectively and add much more value to the patient journey. So why is this important? My mother lives in Katy, Texas, and having been in the USA for over twenty years, she has become very accustomed to US customer service, being treated in a certain way and provided with a level of service. She expects to be called ma'am; she expects the door to be opened for her; she expects shop staff not to be on their phones texting, but to be doing their jobs. There is a clear and obvious link between providing a quality of service that creates positive emotions and the amount you can charge. If you consider that the top 10 best performing brands globally are all American, that deep seated customer service culture that our cousins across the pond have created is clearly working.

What is it that makes a good experience? We talk about positive and negative experiences, but ultimately an experience generates an emotional trigger. Whether that trigger is positive or negative determines how we view that experience. It's no coincidence that the most successful companies with the highest brand value globally are the ones that focus on customer service and put the relationship they have with their customers right at the centre of everything they do. The highest-ranking British company on the list is British Airways, and you also have Coca-Cola, IBM, Microsoft, Google, General Electric, Apple, McDonald's, Intel, Disney, and Hewlett-Packard.

If we take three unrelated brands – BMW, Apple and Starbucks – and ask ourselves, "What is their USP?" we can get a broader insight into how they each put their customer at the centre of the process and create a whole ecosystem and universe around them.

BMW's USP is "The ultimate driving machine", which conveys a clear and concise brand strategy and promise – you will not get anything better. We are the best, and we challenge you to try us and see.

Starbucks is not work, it's not home, it's the "third place", even though it's really just sofas and wi-fi in a shop that sells coffee. It creates an environment you want to stay in; it has great "stick-ability". All of this is because the company has crucially defined its unique selling points. It knows what it's good at.

If you look at Apple's advertising, experience goes right through its heart brand. Sales staff don't talk about RAM and memory size and hard drives; instead, they quote Albert Einstein on their advertising: "*Try not to become a man of success, but rather try to become a man of value.*"

By not talking about specific performance or memory characteristics of its devices, Apple creates a timelessness and moves away from comparisons with PCs and laptops. By not having tills, the shops create an interaction that is intimate compared to many other shopping experiences, not just purchasing consumer technology.

In the end, what these companies do is create compelling customer experiences by using insight and data to meticulously design the journey. Every single interaction and touch point is mapped, and it's executed with absolute ruthlessness, and I believe that the cosmetic surgery industry in the UK can also do this. This simple act of designing the journey will give you a point of difference in the market and clearly separate the good from the bad.

"I'd ask you to sit down, but you're not going to anyway. And don't worry about the vase."

THE ORACLE — THE MATRIX (1999)

"KNOW THYSELF"

've been in the Aesthetic Industry for a few years now, and in that time I've gained some insights into the industry in general which I would like to share with you.

I was once asked to present at a Medical Aesthetic conference in London, and I asked the audience, comprised of medical professionals, to raise their hands if they had designed their USPs, or even simply thought about what made them special and differentiated them in their marketplace.

Not one single hand went up.

That was a bit of a surprise, so I asked another question. "Are you not putting your hand up because you think it's a stupid question or is that because you actually haven't done it?" It was because no one had done it.

No one in that room had clearly defined their USPs, which really surprised me as I don't believe that no one knew what it was that made them special. It was simply that it had not occurred to them to map it out. This is a missed opportunity that has a measurable impact on the actual value of a business.

A business's value is a combination of tangible and intangible assets. Interestingly, if a construction company builds houses, only 84% of that company's value is a tangible asset. If the company is valued at £100 million, £16 million of that value is intangible. It's based around the company's brand promise – the promise made by its USPs.

At the other end of the scale, an advertising agency is pretty much 99% brand promises, 99% intangible value. Even if you're in a business like healthcare or Medical Aesthetics, 50% of your business value is based around your brand promise and your USPs. So if you haven't got clearly defined USPs then you are not realising your business's value to its full potential.

It is important that you recognise your USPs. To help you do this and to pull them out into some real-world scenarios, imagine that someone taps you on the shoulder and asks, "What do you do for a living?"

To find the answer, we need to dig a bit deeper than you may expect and use a process called the Five Whys (or the Whys Guys).

THE FIVE WHYS

It is easy to address a problem or question superficially, but I find the real payoff is a couple of levels down. By asking "Why?", we can lean in to find and understand the core beliefs.

I have always found it challenging when someone asks me, "What do you do?" Suddenly my mind fills with hundreds of things, and for one moment I have a total brain freeze. So I get my own back on the world by asking people the same question and listening to the responses. In the Aesthetic Medicine Industry, invariably the answer is "I'm a cosmetic doctor", "I'm an aesthetic nurse" or "I'm a plastic surgeon".

These are all valid answers, but they are not really USPs. For example, I asked the question, "What do you do for a living?" to my friend and applied the Five Whys to his answer.

"I'm a personal trainer."

Why are you a personal trainer?

"Because I love training in fitness."

Why do you love fitness?

"Because it makes me happy."

Why does it make you happy?

"Because I really love seeing the changes in my clients' experience."

Why do your clients experience change?

"Because I focus on nutrition, physical exercise and life coaching to get results."

Why do you focus on nutrition, physical exercise and life coaching?

"Because it's the most effective way to get results and maintain them."

In a few moments, we uncovered the core belief that drives him and gives him his USP: "I'm a specialist in combining nutrition, physical exercise and life coaching to help my clients achieve rapid results and maintain them."

So if someone asks you, "What do you do for a living?", I believe the question they are actually asking is "What is it that differentiates you from others?"

What I would like you to do now is to pause and complete this little exercise. I use this process for all of my consultation clients; it is hugely effective and only takes a few minutes. You're in the queue at your local cafe or coffee shop, and someone taps you on the shoulder and asks, "What do you do for a living?"

Jot down the first thing that comes into your head.

Now, the tricky bit – apply the Five Whys to your answer.

Your response.

Why?

Why?

Why?

Why?

Why?

Record your responses to make sure that you don't miss anything. I use an app called Rev, which is great for recording audio and allowing you to review it later.

Did you get to the fifth why? If so, what did you discover?

If you didn't, don't worry. It might take you a few attempts to drill down to your core. Just keep trying and you'll uncover that little gem.

The reason that USPs are so important is that differentiating yourself from your competition is all about adding value. The Five Whys give you more ways to describe your USP. Now, on its own, your USP is great, but it's time to introduce the Value Matrix to help get your business to stand out.

Differentiating yourself from your competition is all about adding value, and the stories you tell. The quality of your storytelling is directly related to the cash in your bank. If you tell pants stories, you are going to struggle to get your marketing to work.

In the Value Matrix there are categories of differentiation, going from one to five.

One is a commodity.

A commodity is the base material that is being sold, and is more than likely a raw material, so using a really common example, the commodity here is the humble coffee bean.

Two is the commodity becoming a product. Once you process that raw material, it becomes a product, or goods. The commodity has had value added to it by being refined. In our example, the coffee bean has been roast, and ground, packaged and branded under a trademark such as Lavazza or Douwe Egberts.

The third category is services. The product has had even more value added to it, and a service has been created around it. But who provides the service? You do. You are adding value with your skills, experience, knowledge and understanding. When I begin working with businesses, they are generally around this point in the matrix.

They have a great service, but they don't put the necessary thought into developing their USPs clearly and effectively to add more value to the service so that they create an experience, rather than a service.

Do this well and you will achieve Market Leadership.

Do this well and you will maintain your practice.

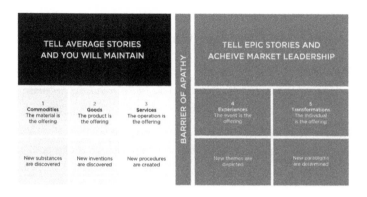

Figure 2: Value Matrix

The fourth category is experience transcends service. When the combination of the service and your own USPs adds enough value to create an experience, and this is well positioned, you begin to break out of the service category. The transition from service to experience takes time, investment and huge commitment, but this is a key stage in the growth of an aesthetic or beauty business, as without a quality experience, you cannot attain the ultimate level.

YOU MUST BE ABLE TO THINK AND ACT AT THIS LEVEL

The fifth category is the individual becoming the offering. This is the ultimate goal. Providing they are of a high enough quality, the preceding four elements will combine in order for you, the individual, to become the offering.

All these elements add value, in turn creating a compelling patient experience and clearly differentiating you from your competition.

It is here that you can charge four times the market rate for your treatments and become a true thought leader in your field.

Not many attain this level as it takes significant investment to create a personal brand as well as a business brand, but by spending some time defining and drawing out your USPs, you will understand fully what it is that makes you different. It could be anything, from your experience, background and knowledge to the quality of your clinic, but you must know thyself.

EXERCISE: KEY VALUES

Here's an exercise you can do (there is also a video for you to follow on the Changing Faces section of the MAETRIX platform and a workbook to help you).

Take ten minutes to write down your three core values. If someone asks you what your three tips for a successful and happy life are, what would you say?

To give you a start, here are the core values for the Aesthetic Entrepreneurs.

- Our Vision – To build successful aesthetic businesses by inspiring the people behind them.

- Be Progressive – Invest in people and ideas.

- Be Powerful – Empower people.

- Be Principled – Stand for something meaningful.

Once you know your key principles, your USPs and business philosophy will become clear, and you'll have created a sense of purpose.

What is your Magnificent Obsession?

My purpose – my "Magnificent Obsession" as I call it – is to help people achieve their goals, regardless of what they are. In turn, they help me achieve mine. This is our bond, our commitment to each other, our big goal, and this can have far reaching results. It is a challenge to stay focused on that big goal. Before we get too far into the method, we need to take a step back and look at a technique to do routinely to keep focused and on message.

That exercise is goal setting.

"See you at the party, Richter!"

DOUGLAS QUAID — TOTAL RECALL (1990)

GOAL SETTING

I use goal setting routinely to help in all of my planning phases, as goals are simply objectives; things I will achieve for the customer, for myself, for my colleagues and for my family.

So what is goal setting?

A quick Google search and the business world will quickly tell you that the best useable method for goal setting is a famous acronym called S.M.A.R.T.

This means:

🚀 Specific

🚀 Measurable

- Achievable

- Realistic

- Timebound

This is a worthy method, but it doesn't work for me because it sets too many limitations. We dream big as children, and nothing is impossible, so why as adults do we believe that "Realistic and Achievable" are the limits of our capabilities? Years ago, when I first entered the corporate world, the SMART acronym was foisted upon me as the goal setting method of choice; however, I felt it was always saying to me "We like you to set goals, but don't be too lofty. We don't want you to get ideas above your station otherwise you may become a troublemaker".

Call me an eternal optimist and unrealistic dreamer, but I saw through this pile of horse manure as quickly as I saw through every sales model (more on that later). The thought of standing in front of my son Isaac and telling him that his goal of being a professional drummer is "unrealistic and unachievable" makes me cringe; it's just something I could never do. I leave that to the naysayers of this world who let their own belief systems cripple their success.

I'm not really concerned about Isaac, as to his credit he'd just tell me that anything is possible, and then, when he's made it, refuse to let me backstage until I'd apologised. If you're struggling for a bit of self-belief, check out the reading list at the end of the chapter for some really inspiring books and resources for those dark days of low motivation.

Incidentally – Saachi & Saachi have "Nothing is Impossible" engraved on the top step of the entrance to their London office, so I guess they'd agree with me, that the SMART acronym is flawed because it prevents you from reaching for the stars and roots your mindset firmly in where you are now, rather than letting you soar and dream.

Luckily, I discovered very soon afterwards the definition of goal setting I still use:

"A committed decision to reach a predetermined, specific goal, combined with a burning desire, followed by immediate, massive action repeated consistently for as long as it takes until your goal is reached."

The author of this quote is one of the most successful people in his generation, an athlete, an actor, a businessman, a politician, and a multi-millionaire. I'll tell you who it is at the end, but let's look again at the key phrases used in this definition:

Committed Decision

Specific Goal

Burning Desire

Immediate MASSIVE Action

Repeated Consistently

For As Long As It Takes

Wow. Even writing them again makes me feel epic. They are incredibly powerful words when you think about it, and actually quite obvious as every day we decide to do something, we set an objective, we act and repeat until it is done, and unfortunately in some parts of the world that goal is simply survival.

So if this is the case, why do we fail? Why do we procrastinate? Why do some people achieve great success and others do not? Why are there so many self-help books?

It's because all are NOT created equal, and the ability to set and achieve goals is what separates us.

Why is goal setting so effective?

Goal setting focuses the subconscious mind on the task in hand and enables us to apply our considerable resourcefulness to achieving it. The old adage of "winners never quit and quitters never win" underpins my philosophy for success.

But what is the difference between success and failure?

A COMMITTED DECISION

Do you CHOOSE to fail because you DECIDE TO STOP trying to succeed? I believe this is the case, it took me four years to get my first company, RCS Consulting, off the ground, and it began on a scrap of paper in January 2008 after an impromptu goal setting session in a car park in Crystal Palace.

I had had enough of the life of a sales representative and was listening to an audiobook of Anthony Robbins' *Awaken the Giant*

---

*"All are NOT created equal,
and the ability to set and
achieve goals is what
separates us."*

Within and was driving my wife crazy with my constant regurgitation of "a decision is not a decision unless you act" (which she felt was pretty obvious), and other highly clichéd soundbites.

But that's the real point, isn't it? It doesn't matter if it is a cliché or not, or you know you should, unless you COMMIT to the decision and act, they're still only words. Goal setting is a HUGE subject, and way too big for us to cover here, which is why we have created a FREE ONLINE GOAL SETTING COURSE for you to access through the MAETRIX!!

The course has been created by my performance coach, Stevie Potter. Yep, coaches have coaches! Stevie is a dentist, entrepreneur, karate black belt and GB triathlete. It's fair to say that she's pretty driven, focussed and has an athlete's discipline. We've been working together for a few years and Stevie has really helped me to focus on my own health and performance as a human being. The truth is that if you are not firing on all cylinders, mentally, physically and emotionally, it's very difficult to achieve your goals.

"There's one common theme with successful people; they all work hard on goal setting properly. But it is an art form and if you've never done it successfully before, it can seem boring, daunting and alien. When you're overwhelmed, worried and confused, you need a plan to keep you moving in the right direction, and that's exactly what goal setting does – or, as I call it, goalSMASHING! I've spent nearly a decade refining my goal smashing process to come up with a strategy that's simple and time effective, and more importantly it works. Every time." Stevie

She's created this short course for you on goal setting, so jump onto the MAETRIX and check it out.

A SPECIFIC GOAL

So let's assume that you have made your Committed Decision to your first specific goal, which should actually be to goal set, grab a nice paper and pen, and write down the following headings:

Career

Family

Adventure

Contribution

EXERCISE: GOALS

Write down 10 SPECIFIC GOALS under each heading and let your mind soar – in this life we are constrained only by ourselves, so really go for it! I write down "Orbit the Earth" and "Climb Everest" under Adventure every goal-setting day.

Next thing is to RANK YOUR GOALS in order of importance to you on a scale of 1 to 10. In 2008 I wrote that an MBA was less important to me than the respect of the industry and my customers. I still don't have an MBA because it is no longer relevant for me, but respect always is.

Burning Desire

Everyone has to do things that bore the pants off them. While I cast my mind back to the last instalment of the Twilight series and immediately my motivation to do anything other than laugh at buff wolf boy and pouty vampires is lost. However, your new goal MUST be worth the effort, this MUST become a "magnificent obsession" and if your enthusiasm to achieve it needs to be mustered, then review its importance. Which would you rather have, infectious enthusiasm or a polite shrug?

What's the point of working hard to learn how to dance if you hate dancing? You'll quit and feel like you have failed when all you did was choose the wrong goal. I wanted to climb Everest, but I don't have a burning desire to do it – my friend Tarka L'Herpiniere did, and he has now summited three times! In fact, he should probably be writing this.

Take IMMEDIATE and MASSIVE ACTION

I love this bit – Immediate and Massive action, not tomorrow but NOW. Medical Aesthetics is packed full of entrepreneurial business owner operators and it's great. The simple fact that you are reading this means that the streak of entrepreneurship runs deep in you and you want to get things done. However, sometimes the burst of enthusiasm does wane and we need a little kick. I just think "I must move this rock now and it must move a long way"; often this is in the early stage of our planning process and gets us a good head start. My father calls it "Breaking the back of a job", by putting a massive amount of effort into it at the early stages so you are always ahead.

Repeated Consistently

Now, this is the real challenge, isn't it? Going to the gym, dieting, learning a language or instrument, this is the phase of goal setting that you WILL fall down on, because we are creatures of habit, and our default habit is to make excuses to not do things. If you've been not doing things for most of your life, it's going to be a tough habit to break! Apparently, it takes 30 days for habit forming activities to embed themselves and probably five minutes to break them, and often we take on too much in one go. Change your life and habits one at a time, and train yourself to succeed and achieve your goals.

For As Long As It Takes

Remember the final part – for as long as it takes. It took me four years to achieve the goals I wrote in Crystal Palace, and as Tarks will tell you, climbing Everest isn't something you can just decide to do on a Tuesday afternoon and squeeze in after the gym (well you can, you'll just die a slow painful death, which is kind of the ultimate failure).

So, who is the genius who set me on the way to independence, and becomes the strange focus on a Friday morning?

Albert Einstein? Vince Lombardi? Richard Branson?

Nope.

Arnold Schwarzenegger.

Arnie arrived in the USA from Austria and simply wrote his goals for the year on index cards. He looked at them every day and made a conscious effort to achieve them. By the time he was 30 he was a millionaire, long before his Hollywood movie days.

So take your time, focus on what you want to achieve, be sure you want it and enjoy the ride.

If Arnold can do it, why can't you?

Just in case your mind is a bit blown, here's the link to the MAETRIX once again.

Like I said, I'll be back.

Let's look in detail over the next few chapters at some of my learning experiences and some Key Mistakes. But before we do, we need to explore how I actually got here.

PART 2

WHERE DO YOU
WANT TO GO?

*"Mama always said life was like a box
of chocolates. You never know
what you're gonna get."*

FORREST GUMP – FORREST GUMP (1994)

MY JOURNEY

My journey into Medical Aesthetics happened completely by accident; however, I can follow the gentle guiding hand of serendipity from a rugby match in 1997 to me being late for a train to London in 2003.

I took a train from Reading to Plymouth on 17th June 1991 aged 17 years, one month and one week, and joined the Royal Navy. I was absolutely terrified. I was still very much a kid, but I had been fixed on joining up since I was about five, as one of my mother's school friends, Beau, had joined up and I vividly remember the uniform, the adoring looks from ladies, the jealous looks from men and falling over his kit bag when going out of the house on the way to school. The fact that I wanted so badly to join the RN, and they took you with practically no qualifications at all, meant that it didn't really matter that I also failed all of my GCSE exams. The Navy didn't seem to care if you were not academic, so why should I?

The next seven years are a bit of a whirlwind, but it kind of went like this: June 1991 – HMS Raleigh, HMS Ark Royal, Bosnia, HMS Invincible, Bosnia, HMS Nelson, lots of rugby, HMS Montrose, South Atlantic, HMS Dryad, more rugby, anterior cruciate ligament, college. November 1998 – Discharged.

Now, I learnt a huge amount in the Armed Forces, and those of you reading this who have served will understand what I mean, but the biggest lesson I was given was by a chief petty officer at the end of my Part Two training, this is after your initial Basic or Part One training.

Part One is where you are just given an 8-week character and maturity test, of which I'm still not sure how I got through, and you are put under a massive amount of pressure. I'm not ashamed to say that I found it incredibly hard. Everyone struggles with something, be it naval discipline, maintaining your kit or fitness, and, for me, I really struggled keeping my kit together, and I was on the brink of being booted out altogether a couple of times; however, I was pretty good at rugby, which helped to sway certain things in my direction, and I was selected for the Navy Colts Rugby Squad before I'd even finished my Part Two training.

Part Two was intense but not quite so full on as Basic, but even still you needed to keep on top of things. But I was enjoying it by this point and just before we finished Part Two and were dispatched on the next leg of our training journey, we had our final reviews to see how we had performed overall, and I was given a lesson I have never forgotten.

I was called into the "Chiefs Office". It was just like being called to see the headmaster, and the chiefs office overlooked the parade ground. Chief petty officers in the Royal Navy are the glue that hold it all together. They provide the leadership, discipline and training for pretty much everyone in the Navy, including the Officer Corps – a fact they are not scared of sharing with you at any opportunity. I remember smiling at the class of new recruits being verbally brutalised on the Parade Ground, with some classic drill instructor lines like, "there is a village somewhere missing an idiot", and "if the Navy doesn't work, you have a great career ahead as a paperweight", and so on. Amazing how quickly you forget which is your left and right when you're being bellowed at. It's probably classed as bullying now, but in 1991 most of the instructors at HMS Raleigh had served in the Falklands War. The Navy lost four ships in the conflict and the impact of that were plain for all to see. You can understand why they really didn't give much of a toss about political correctness.

I was called in, I sat down and was given my training feedback, which was on the whole pretty good. Basically, it said I was a bright kid and worked quite hard when I needed to, which to be fair was better than my school reports, and Mum would have liked that, so I was quite happy.

Then this chief leans across his desk, looks me in the eye and says: "The Navy, young man, is just like life. It will give you nothing for nothing. Take what you can, when you can."

He then leans back, shuffles the papers, looks up and says:

"Well? Bugger off then!"

That comment has rattled around my head for years and years, trying to make sense of it. Knowing chief petty officers as I do now, it was something that was said a thousand times to a thousand recruits passing through, but it had a huge impact on me as it has given me a healthy attitude to risk.

I had a great time, and left the Navy in 1998, with a hatred of the Middle Watch, Air Defence Exercises, and the South West Approaches. I now look back on my time with some fondness and warmth, but the reality is that I was ready for a new challenge, and after a particularly painful knee injury put me shoreside and out of action, I spent the last two years of my service based just outside of Portsmouth, I went to college and got myself into the University of Portsmouth, aged 24, to study in the emerging field of New Media and Creative Technologies. Ever since I was a small child I've been fascinated by film and storytelling, and the evidence of that is here in your hand. Every chapter begins with a quote from one of my favourite films. I did once have ambitions of being in the movie industry and working in digital special effects, and my degree was a step on that journey. Truth be known, I realised very early that I didn't have the talent to compete with the coders and maths whizzes that were really going for it, but I was very good at building and leading teams. So my role came managing projects and acting as the course representative to the board of studies. I graduated with a "Desmond (2:2)" in 2002, aged 28, and was living in Brighton, a triumphant return to the glorious South Coast of the UK, from living with my father in Bristol. I graduated, pumped up and ready to take on the commercial world; however, I was completely unprepared for the Dot.Com crash. Go to uni, leave uni, no jobs in your chosen field, the Royal Navy careers office was beginning to look very, very attractive.

I eventually got a job in the creative industries in July 2002. Well, I say the Creative Industries, at a stretch it was, but really I was a sales rep for a print company. I was commuting to Shoreditch from Brighton, and I felt like I had the world at my feet – a job in London, a flat in Brighton with my girlfriend, the sun was shining, I had the beach at the weekend and the gentle cooling breeze of the sea. Life was good.

Fast forward to the winter of 2002, I had no girlfriend, that gentle summer breeze turned into a flesh-stripping hurricane, the commute was a life filled with 5AM starts and overcrowded trains, and my sales role was soul destroying. My dream had become my winter of discontent – the Royal Navy careers office was beginning to look very, very attractive again.

It was then when I had one of those "character building mistakes" for which I was ripped apart, and to be fair, it was another valuable lesson.

I had just won a really solid blue-chip client; however, in my excitement I made a bit of a howler on the proposal document and ultimately quoted the cost price and forgot to mark it up.

I'd been working on this project for weeks, and it was all my own work, from cold call, initial meeting, pitch and then through to proposal, and I was really proud of this one. Over time, I had built up a really strong relationship with the client, by listening to what they wanted, but guiding them back to a core point, and thinking about what their customers valued about them. I was basically helping them to focus on what their USPs were and how to communicate them to their customers, (although I didn't know that at the time).

I had also worked to get this client to focus on investment rather than cost, and then gone and completely blown it with a simple mistake.

Now rather than ask me how I was going to fix it, the managing director chose to shout at your humble narrator in an open-plan office in front of the entire company. I was completely unprepared for this, and even though I like to think that I'm a pretty robust character, it really shook me up. I think it was Dale Carnegie that wrote something like "if you want to create a hatred that burns for 1,000 years, publicly humiliate someone in front of his peers", and he was bang on. I'm pissed off to this day about that as I'm not sure what the point of it was. In reality, all it achieved was make him look like a dickhead and me look for another job, as when all you can think about is putting someone through a wall, it's probably a good time to leave.

"Hi, is that the Royal Navy? I've made a terrible mistake. Can I come back?"

Obviously, I decided not to go back, but I felt I was getting nothing for a lot, time to change – and serendipity finally agreed. Serendipity made me late for the train from Brighton, I can't remember exactly what happened, but in that carriage was an old friend from my home town, who I'd not seen for a good few years. We agreed to meet up for a drink and before you know it I had ditched my flat and was living in his spare room. That chance meeting set the course for the next 10 years of my life. We've been to each other's weddings, watched each other's children grow and to this day remain very close friends.

At the time, he just happened to be working for a small bio tech that sold a Hyaluronic Acid Filler, a sales manager role at his company came up, I went for it, and the rest is history. So what does this actually have to do with this book?

Well, nothing or everything, it depends on your point of view. This is either a self-indulgent chapter in a book that tells you nothing you don't already know, or an insight into the mind and perspective of a fellow business professional.

It's up to you, but what I'm going to do is keep on trying to win, trying to smile and stay positive. I'll just keep swimming.

This book represented another opportunity to take advantage of, and ultimately that is what that chief petty officer was trying to tell me.

The simple truth is that it's not just life, but everything that is like the Navy, take advantage of every opportunity that presents itself, otherwise it will give you nothing for nothing.

Take what you can, when you can.

When I look back on this pivotal period in my life, which was essentially me transitioning my entire career, what always stands out is that I was consolidating knowledge and experience into one thing – helping people tell stories. We are always communicating to potential customers, existing customers, customers of customers, partners, potential partners and building relationships on some level.

One key thing I also learnt was to keep things really, really simple, from coaching rugby through to business. For example, on Sunday mornings when I was coaching kids' rugby, I'd distil the game for them, because if you think about the game of rugby, at its heart it is very simply, "Run forwards, pass backwards".

I try to apply this same simplicity to my business and products, so for me as an individual, I want to be innovative, big and bold, professionally edgy, fearless and funny, and at its heart I simply want to help people achieve their goals.

I see so many aesthetic business owners make the same mistakes over and over again and they completely hamper the business growth and development. Yes, we must learn by doing, but save yourself some time and stress, read the next chapter and eliminate these common mistakes from your life.

"Oh yes, the past can hurt. But you can either run from it or learn from it."

RAFIKI – THE LION KING (1994)

THE SIX KEY MISTAKES

Most businesses in the aesthetic and beauty sectors make the same Seven Key Mistakes. Now this is not an exhaustive list of mistakes by any means, but over the years of working in aesthetic businesses, I have seen the same common issues many times and these mistakes will prevent you from attaining the high levels you aspire to.

MISTAKE NUMBER 1 – Not being authentic

MISTAKE NUMBER 2 – Telling the wrong stories

MISTAKE NUMBER 3 – Not enough understanding of the client's problem

MISTAKE NUMBER 4 – Not creating an experience

MISTAKE NUMBER 5 – Trying to skip the struggle

MISTAKE NUMBER 6 – Starting too big

In his book, *The 7 Habits of Highly Effective People*, Stephen Covey references the importance of being Principle Centred.

If you have read it you will know what I'm talking about; if you haven't read it, I highly recommend that you do. Being Principle Centred simply means having a core philosophy. I read it in 2011, and one of my core principles is to inspire people – which is something I try to do every day.

But before I get stuck into humiliating everyone who has ever made mistakes, I would like to confess something: I have made every single one of these mistakes, sometimes more than once and sometimes a few at the same time. They're inevitable. I hate making mistakes, and as I'm someone who loathes the feeling of failure, you would be forgiven for believing that I would actively avoid them. However, the interesting thing is that I have learnt not to avoid making mistakes; I just make sure I learn the lessons from them. This is a total paradox. In the UK, especially in the corporate world, mistakes are perceived as hugely negative, and the process can often be quite a painful experience.

I have been chewed out many times for making mistakes, and in all cases no one actually died, lost money or was in any way inconvenienced. All that had actually happened is that I'd tried to do something a different way. By now you'll gather I'm a bit of a free thinker, and I don't much like being told what to do, but I do enjoy learning and I learn fast, so always get a huge amount from these experiences.

The first lesson I learnt was a principle that has stood me in good stead for many years. I learnt how to spot and minimise the most destructive business relationship you can possibly have, and one that if you encourage too many can rip your business apart.

I am talking about the Bears, and we'll explore them in a later chapter.

I was an ambitious guy, and I had longed for the title of director or vice president on the business card, but I eventually realised what I might have to become to achieve that and by working for someone else, you're not really a director or a VP, you're an employee, plain and simple.

Now, there is nothing wrong with that, if that's what you want to be; however, I wanted more. I wanted to push boundaries, try different things and experience more variety in my working life.

The other lesson in those uncomfortable experiences is that innovation can never come from a position of comfort, they are mutually exclusive, and by reading this book you are clearly looking for new ways to achieve something, and credit to you because true innovation rarely comes from inside a host organisation, it's not possible – it's too sanitised and comfortable. If you look at your iPhone, a huge number of the feats in that device have been acquired or bought by Apple, not developed by them. For example, the magnifying effect that you get when you hold down on a word? Not invented by Apple. It was created by a guy called Bas Ording.

When they were looking for people to design the graphical interface for Apple's new operating system, Jobs got an email from a young man and invited him in. The applicant was nervous, and the meeting did not go well.

Later that day, Jobs bumped into him, dejected, sitting in the lobby. The guy asked if he could just show him one of his ideas, so Jobs looked over his shoulder and saw a little demo of a way to fit more icons in the dock at the bottom of a screen.

When the guy moved the cursor over the icons crammed into the dock, the cursor mimicked a magnifying glass and made each icon balloon bigger.

Jobs hired him on the spot, the feature became part of IOS, and the designer went on to design such things as inertial scrolling for multi-touch screens (the feature that makes the screen keep gliding for a moment after you've finished swiping).

That young designer was Bas Ording.

Bas now holds the position of User Interface Designer at Apple. You simply cannot innovate without making mistakes, and in my experience in corporations there are often too many people who fear making them.

Steve Jobs said, "Stay foolish", and I agree. Keep pushing, innovate, try something and make a mistake. There are no mistakes in life really, just opportunities to learn. How do I know? You're reading a book about my mistakes, and if I can learn from them, anyone can. My software business failed, mainly because I had absolutely no idea how to build a software system or run a business, but I went for it anyway.

Happily, Aesthetic Entrepreneurs has grown rapidly because I learnt from those mistakes.

No crazy ideas? No mistakes? No Aesthetic Entrepreneurs.

However, I do see the same mistakes repeated over and over again. Occasionally I come across a company that seems to defy logic – it provides poor service, charges high prices, yet still manages to have a booming business. There are exceptions to every rule, but eventually they will get found out.

They always do.

"We are who we choose to be."

GREEN GOBLIN – SPIDER-MAN (2002)

MISTAKE NUMBER 1 – NOT BEING AUTHENTIC

Sometimes, out of nowhere, an opportunity will present itself, and from that opportunity another, and another. Often, we try to reach the end far too quickly and not allow things to evolve. The simplest thing to do in any new opportunity is always to find the simplest next step. If there is no logical next step, then there's no reason for a business relationship. If there is something, then you seize on that opportunity and take it one step forward.

The home runs and quantum leaps come once in a blue moon, so just take it one step at a time and eventually, after you've taken enough steps, you'll get to your goal. You will also grow in confidence. It's exhausting trying to leap, so just go from step to step and eventually you'll build something, and that began for me on one summer's day in London.

One of the major challenges for me in the City of London is actually finding the correct door number for a building. It's like a game created hundreds of years ago that has been designed to totally infuriate me, by putting an address in the wrong street. For example, 32 Threadneedle Street is actually next to 5, not 30. (If you're not from the UK, sorry, but this will help you at some point.)

This whole area around St Paul's was engulfed in flames in the Great Fire of London in 1666. During the rebuilding, the planners had a great opportunity to make London a bit like New York, with an ordered block system and make things really easy to find. But someone somewhere said, "Nah, that's a terrible idea. Who wants to do that? Let's make sure that in 300 years' time no one can find anywhere. Also, triangular buildings are cool and street numbers that make no sense whatsoever are definitely the way to go".

Anyway, I wasn't exactly dressed for your typical business meeting. In fact, you could say I wasn't dressed for business at all in my casual jeans and t-shirt. Having recently spent a large amount of time with lawyers and bankers, you see the suited masses everywhere and begin to feel that you should fit in. Miriam, my voice of reason, is going crazy. Conversations with the voice of reason, also known as your internal dialogue, are much more fun if you give that voice a name, and I have named mine "Miriam" in honour of my great grandmother, a wonderfully sensible woman who taught me that if you wear a coat indoors you won't feel the benefit, that eating your breadcrusts will make your hair curl, that swans can break your leg, that lemons dry your blood, and only bikers, sailors or fallen women have tattoos.

"Put on a shirt, cover up those tattoos, you ruffian. What would the neighbours say?" You may be thinking, why today? Why out of all these days did I decide to go to an important meeting casual.

But why not? Absolutely why not.

Then, when the door of opportunity presents itself, you'll give it one hell of a boot and you see what's on the other side. So maybe, me not buying the shirt is a bit that differentiates me from everybody else, and if a few tattoos offend him then who cares! I was a sailor, after all.

Now, where the hell is 32 Threadneedle Street? A few years ago, I probably would've gone and bought a shirt. This time, I said "no". I did not buy a shirt. I went in as I was, and frankly it was so bloody hot he should have been grateful I was wearing clothes at all. Guess what? No one batted an eyelid. I guess a few naked men had already been in that day.

Something in me changed that day and win, lose or draw with that meeting, I felt like I had taken a real step forward. We live in the social media age where everyone has the right to show the world what they want them to see through their own personal window, but what is shown is often a cultivated, carefully controlled image, in essence, your "brand". You only see the success, not the failures; the wealth, not the poverty; the car, not the debt; the material, not the soul.

That's not authentic.

Authenticity is what's real; it's hard-earned insight. My insight into not buying that shirt, while it may seem like a trivial thing, was a huge step for me. I have been conditioned to wear a uniform at work from the age of 17. First in the Royal Navy and then as a sales rep, putting the shirt and tie on every day and grabbing my briefcase. My briefcase was just a crutch, something to carry around with you to give you confidence that you were a real businessman. Most of the time I couldn't really tell you what I had in it, but it told the world I had confidence that I was up to the job. And, just like that, I didn't need to dress like that to prove anything, because I finally had the belief – the imposter had gone, allowing myself to feel like a leading figure in my field, a published author and award winner, however I was dressed. Recognising that we are creating something that is actually really innovative and really disruptive. I am my brand, my brand is me. My brand, my rules. You are your brand, your brand is you.

Your brand, your rules. What you see is what you get, and it doesn't wear a shirt. It has tattoos. It's a little bit of rough around the edges. It likes to be bold, likes to push things, to test theories, to get shit horribly wrong and to do Facebook Live videos.

Recognise and accept that you and your business are linked, and be yourself. It's incredibly liberating, and you will be far happier and much more successful as a result. There are far too many vanilla businesses out there in our market, and you need to set yourself apart. Gaining clarity was the first step that I had to take on this journey. I needed to understand more about who I was, who I was serving and what the problems they had actually were. I felt that, because I'd been out of the loop and had my head in the weeds for so long, I'd lost touch with my own market. In reality, the problems were exactly the same – low pricing, struggling to get clients – and I realised that we were still telling the wrong stories. You need to be authentic and create experiences and transformations.

*"There's nothing in the world
more powerful than a good story."*

**TYRION LANNISTER — GAME OF THRONES,
EPISODE 73 "THE IRON THRONE" (2019)**

MISTAKE NUMBER 2 — TELLING THE WRONG STORIES

Humans are attracted to a good story like a moth to a flame, and we need to change the way that we talk about ourselves and our businesses. Essentially, it's about the stories we tell, and you can use the Value Matrix from Chapter 3 to help you do this.

You've got a scale from one to five where one is the lowest value story and five is the highest value story. People tend to stop around three on that scale – Services.

They talk primarily about treatments and products. If you Google your competitors and have a look at their marketing, you will see that many of them are talking about the exact same things as you and that's because you have reached the "barrier of apathy". To break through that barrier, and not be vanilla, and tell epic stories, you have to invest time, energy and money.

Those stories are about the experiences you provide, how you are changing people's lives, how you as an individual are doing really cool things. When you tell epic stories you become a leader. If there's one thing you should take away from this it's to talk more about experiences and transformations and less about goods and services – I promise you'll make more money if you do.

Need some more inspiration?

Tell these stories.

TELL THE STORY ABOUT YOU BEING A LEADER

There's no room for shrinking violets in this new economy, not if you want to make it through. You've got to be super proactive (even though I hate to use the word "super"). You've got to be the voice of your business. You need to step up because, if you're not going to be the one who does it, no one else will. You need to be a leader and take a stand in your community. Is there a time when you have stood up for what you believe? Is there a time when you have turned a client away for not being the right fit? That is the story to tell. Demonstrate that you are a trusted voice by being online, being proactive, talking about these experiences and encouraging engagement. These are the things that are highly prized right now and will definitely be valuable in the future.

TELL THE STORY ABOUT YOUR PERSONAL BRAND

The highest value is where people come to see you as an individual. When people connect with you as a person. With Aesthetic Entrepreneurs, I talk almost entirely about experiences and transformations. Yes, I talk about the products that we provide, the services that we provide, but more often than not, I'll be talking heavily about what those do and how they impact people's businesses and people's lives.

It's not just about your business, it's also about you as an individual and your personal brand has to shine through because when you do that, you can start to create a community. Having a community is an incredible thing because when you have that you have created your own market. Some clients say to me, "I want to create a personal brand, but I'm reluctant to do so because I don't want to sell my personal life like many do", and that's a great point to raise. We assume that creating a personal brand means we're selling our personal lives, but we are not, the two are different. Your personal brand is about your vision, your values and your belief systems as a professional within your business, nothing more.

If you want to keep your family and what you do in the evening out of that then you can, everyone's entitled to a private life. For me, it's about vision, values and principles – what I stand for – and sharing all of those as a human being. What you've got to bear in mind is that marketing is all about communication from one human being to another. If you try and do it hidden behind a brand, you miss that vital connection. Even Apple at one point was just two guys – Steve Jobs and Steve Wozniak – that was it. People engaged with them as human beings. The brand didn't come until much, much later. Share what you're comfortable with and nothing more.

Anyone who works with me or knows me will know that I can be very blunt, honest and direct, so I am going to be so here. Who cares? If people judge you, that's their problem. Who gives a shit? The people you should care about are those who are working with you. If I put something out there, 50% of people might not agree with me or even like me. Fine, I don't care. I used to. I used to deeply care what people thought of me. Now, I don't, and there's a reason for it. It's because the people who don't care about me don't help. I'm not going to listen to them. It's kind of like, "Why listen to people that you wouldn't take advice from?" Now, I'm not saying that is easy, it's not, it's challenging and it's going to knock you right outside of your comfort zone. Your comfort zone's going to grow a mile wide. It's a mindset thing. But you are going to get used to that fear, that little bit of a sick feeling that you have. Live with it. It's going to be there for years. It's just called being an entrepreneur. Being an entrepreneur is a vocation. It's incredibly rewarding, but also incredibly challenging.

TELL THE STORY ABOUT HOW YOU BUILD RELATIONSHIPS

To generate trust with a particular person the first thing we need to be is likeable. This is why sharing your personal brand is really important, because without sharing these parts of your personal brand, it's difficult to generate trust. If it's difficult to generate trust, it's difficult to get clients.

If your clients trust you to solve their problems, you will never need to sell anything and that essentially is the crux of it all. Trust is a currency that will be in massive demand in the new economy, so the quicker you can build it and the stronger it is, the more revenue you will generate and the more your business will grow. All this is leading to the main point that the way that we do business has changed. You need to change, and I want you to start right here.

The next thing is authority. Who are you and why do you know what you know? Everybody wants to be in safe hands, right? Most people want to be with someone who knows what they're talking about, has demonstrable success and has a proven track record, so you need to demonstrate those things.

Finally, it's about credibility. You need to be credible. For me, that also means not making outlandish claims. Be humble, honest and direct, but also communicate what you do well. This is the core of ethical businesses.

TELL THE STORY ABOUT HOW YOU CREATE CONTENT

What you need to understand is that in this new economy you are now 60% practitioners and 40% media producers. If you want to own it, you've got to think like this. Now, you might be thinking, where'd he get that stat from? Well, I made it up. It's completely fabricated, but it's probably closer to what you should be doing than where you are now. Now you are probably more like 95% practitioner, 5% media producer, and this has to change. It's not optional anymore. We've got to be proactive, we've got to be online. This is the way the world is. So, how can I make it easy? Well, the easiest way is to break it down into three parts.

1. **Strategy** – Who am I talking to, what am I saying and what do I want them to do with the information I've given them?

2. **Production –** What is the best way of getting that message across?

   For me, media or content, if some people would want to call it that way, comes in four different guises: visual (video or image), audio (podcasting is massive at the moment), written (blogging or straight up posts), or interactive (quizzes and things like that). Those are generally the four flavours it comes in. Decide which one you want to use.

3. **Distribution –** How are you going to share it? Where is it going? Who's it going to? What is it you're putting out there? This is when it comes down to thinking about the social media channels you want to use, for example, Instagram, Facebook, Twitter or LinkedIn. If you do those things and break it down like that – strategy, production and distribution – you'll immediately be more effective.

   However – yes, there is a however – none of this works unless you're actually creating the content in the first place. So you can have the strategy, the production mechanism and the distribution channels, but if you're not actually making it, then it's utterly pointless anyway. The reason your marketing is failing is because you are hiding. You need to stop hiding.

EXERCISE – STOP HIDING!

You are talented professionals, you know what you're doing, you're respected, but you've got to show the world how brilliant you are. I want you to stop hiding right now so it's selfie time. I want you to take a selfie and put it somewhere in the world. I don't care where it goes. If you're in the Aesthetic Entrepreneurs group, it can go in there. It can go on your own Facebook page. It can go anywhere. I don't care, so long as you put the hashtag #aestheti-centrepreneurs.

I really encourage you to do this. You are an entrepreneur and entrepreneurs are bold, fearless people, so be bold and be fearless and post that selfie right now. I won't know if you have done it or not, but you will and that's all that matters.

"Too many mind."

NOBUTADA – THE LAST SAMURAI (2003)

MISTAKE NUMBER 3 – NOT ENOUGH UNDERSTANDING OF THE CLIENT'S PROBLEM

The first, and probably key rule of business, is that you need to create a product or service people love enough to tell others about it. Without this, you have nothing, and yet it's incredible how little thought new business owners actually put into the creation of their services.

We are all in the business of problem solving. The reason you are reading this book is not out of a very generous desire to give me money (although thank you if you did), your goal of reading this book is to solve a particular problem that you have. If you read this and I help, then you will feel that you've had value for money, and I hope that I as the author know enough about the problems you have to be able to give insight in these pages.

Fortunately, I'm pretty sure I know how to help you, and this is a mistake that many people make and I'm going to stop you from doing it right now. On the flip side, if you get this right, it will have a huge transformative impact on your business, and that is to properly understand who you serve and connect with them on an emotional level. If you want to connect emotionally with your particular client, you need to understand them, who they are, what hopes and dreams they have, what challenges they have, and how you can help them to either solve those problems or achieve those goals.

Let me give you an example. A few years ago, I was invited to speak at a well-known conference on the topic of "Why you should work with a Business Consultant". "Excellent", I thought to myself, "what a great opportunity to promote myself and drive my business forward." However, it turned out to be the worst presentation I have ever done, and appearing at that conference probably did me more harm than good.

I made two absolutely massive mistakes, which meant that I really struggled during the preparation for the congress and actually during the presentation itself, and I still see Medical Aesthetic professionals making exactly the same mistakes. Have you done the same?

My first massive mistake was that I didn't focus on what I was good at, my core offering.

Your core offering is at the heart of your business. It's your essence, your passion, it's you without the bullshit. Essentially it's what you would do if you didn't need any money. Much of business is actually centred on problem solving. Our customers feel a pain, and we create products and services to take away that pain. This design process is a constant game. If I didn't have to earn a crust, would I become an airline pilot? A fireman? A doctor? No, I would continue to find ways to help you guys get clarity, feel more confident in business and achieve your goals. So, if that desire to serve is firmly at my core, why on earth did I waffle on about technology and apps? Because I thought it would make me look credible, but it actually did the opposite.

Without being able to tap-in to my core, during the preparation I put together what can only be described as dull as shit, and what contributed to the next mistake is I knew it too.

I know it sounds ridiculous now, but at the time I was so enthusiastic that I really wanted to nail the presentation, I didn't actually think about who I was presenting to, and what they wanted to know. The next massive mistake was that I didn't respect my USPs. Your USPs are the key to understanding what makes you different from your competition, and being able to communicate what makes you different and why you are the best is the key to your business growth. I should have asked myself, "Does this topic support my USPs, does it drive my business forward or is it going to confuse things?"

By the time the presentation came I was in a perfect storm of total confusion, no real passion for the subject and nerves, combined in the form of rubbish content, no real point and a poor delivery.

"If you focus on how YOU serve your clients and the problem you solve, you WILL be more successful and find yourself enjoying your work more."

With 20/20 hindsight, I really wish I had the confidence to say "Thanks for the opportunity; however, I specialise in helping to build aesthetic businesses by inspiring the entrepreneurs behind them". Had I held myself true to the problem I solve for people, this would have changed the subject for the talk, or removed me from it. Either way it would have saved me from the humbling experience of crashing and burning in front of a room full of people!

We are often far too afraid to focus down, and niche to solve a problem. By trying to do too much and cover too many bases we dilute ourselves. At the end of the day, we MUST come back to one key fact, which is as entrepreneurs our primary role is to solve problems for our clients, and if we don't have a deep understanding of what those problems are, we will never fully engage with our ideal clients, and we never realise our full potential. We cover this more in a later chapter, but for now just remember that you can't be all things to all people, that's a job for God.

"Too many mind" is a favourite quote I often use with people, and mutter to myself sometimes. It's from *The Last Samurai*, a 2003 film starring Tom Cruise, and is a cue to regain a mental state free of distraction; focussed, and uncluttered.

In the film, *The Last Samurai*, Capt. Nathan Algren (Tom Cruise) is an American military officer hired by the Emperor of Japan to train the country's first army in the art of modern warfare.

The storyline takes place in 19th century Japan during the Meiji Restoration. Captain Algren is taken captive by Samurai and held in their village. They treat him very well and he is free to walk around the village, only with an escort, and observe their customs and lifestyle. During his time with the Samurai, Algren trains as a Samurai, and as one would expect is given a good whooping. Time after time he is beaten with a bokken, until one of the young Samurai named Nobutada (played by Shin Koyamada) decides to help him.

Nobutada: "Please forgive... too many mind."

Algren: "Too many mind?"

Nobutada: "Hai (yes). Mind the sword, mind the people watch (watching), mind the enemy, too many mind. No mind."

Algren: "No mind?"

Nobutada: "No mind."

Algren takes a moment to understand the meaning of the advice given, and is then, in true Hollywood style, no longer a whipping boy and the match ends in a draw.

Just like Algren, we all have too many minds, which flows into everything we do – home, life and business. "Too many minds", "not enough hours in the day", "I'm too busy". These are lies we tell ourselves. The truth is that there are 24hrs in the day, 168 in one week, and we all have the same amount, but the difference is on what you focus on in those hours.

If you focus on how YOU serve your clients and the problem you solve, you WILL be more successful and find yourself enjoying your work more. Of course, you can eventually diversify and add treatments to create programmes, but they must solve a meaningful problem, and that is what you must always be mindful of.

"I've always treated every man the same: just as another, future customer."

**CHAMLEE THE UNDERTAKER
– THE MAGNIFICENT SEVEN (1960)**

MISTAKE NUMBER 4 – NOT CREATING AN EXPERIENCE

If we want to own this new experience economy, we need to leverage experience over price. I keep talking about value but that's what it's all about. I've long believed that people in the aesthetics community in the UK undervalue themselves massively. They undercharge horrendously and don't make any money. For me, providing high-quality services at a high cost is the best mechanism. Why? Because if we can serve more people in the best possible way, then we need to be rewarded for that, which means we need to charge appropriately for it.

I've been around doctors, nurses and plastic surgeons for many years, in varying roles in this industry, from an area sales manager, product specialist, key account manager, and a business consultant. I've worked across pretty much every speciality there is and worked with businesses ranging from a single independent nurse to the biggest and baddest multi-site chains in the sector, and what this experience has taught me, what it has convinced me, without the shadow of a doubt, is that selling and purchasing on price is a terrible, terrible decision.

Why is it so bad?

You must sell The Experience, not the cost, as you are probably not charging enough as it is.

Economic headwinds touch us all, and it's been a very challenging few years to say the least.

As things begin to brighten after the storm and show positivity, will there be a cultural legacy from the pandemic? You betcha! The British will finally refuse to accept poor quality and poor service. My big takeaway from the last few years is how intolerant I have become of mediocrity. The fact that I have to work hard for my money means that I am loathe to just hand it over to someone who thinks that charging four pounds for a cup of coffee is acceptable. Starbucks, we pay our taxes, you pay yours.

Maybe it's because I'm getting older and more grumpy, but I look around and I do see a pattern emerging, and major businesses worldwide are focussing heavily on "customer experiences". The cynic in me is saying that plain ol' customer services simply isn't cutting the mustard, so let's change the job title from "Customer

Services Rep" to "Customer Experience Advisor" and carry on as normal with the same level of service.

As recent personal experiences would suggest, some companies view this as a valid strategy; however, later I provide some examples of this being executed well.

So, in your business, is it still "Customer Services Team" or is it "Your Customer Experience Team"? Well, funky job titles aside, I do think that if executed with excellence, a focus on customer experience is the right thing to do.

We work with lots of start-up businesses and focus on business models and creating a powerful customer experience, as well as generating profit. Why? Because a true start-up business, creating a unique product, will have a small number of customers, so it's easier to manage them, and an influential evangelistic early adopter is worth its weight in gold.

However, once the business becomes established, it becomes easy to forget about the customer experience and focus purely on the numbers; you forget the thing that made you successful in the first place.

I advise you to not only look at the finances, but also use customer satisfaction as measures of business success, as recessions tend to clean out poorly performing companies. Your business may look strong on paper, but if you're not looking after your customer, eventually they will punish you.

So think about your staff. What are their roles? Is your business focussed to welcome, to smile, to engage, or does it appear austere and unfriendly?

DON'T USE THE GOLDFISH PRINCIPLE

I recently read an article on LinkedIn by a management consultant called Don Peppers, who has coined the phrase "The Goldfish Principle" to describe business memory. Some species of tropical fish have no territorial memory and are therefore more than happy to circle a bowl as there is always something very interesting to see, think Dory in *Finding Nemo*. (Just keep swimming...)

Customers are not tropical fish, and calling someone three times to say "we're just calling to see if you're interested in our latest promotion", is The Goldfish Principle in action. When said customer comes in to claim the latest promotion, having no idea what they're talking about, is also The Goldfish Principle and an example of poor execution of a marketing plan.

Try to operate on the principle that whoever you are talking to deserves your FULL attention; if they're a customer, they're your best one. If they're not, they soon will be. With the technology available to you to provide customer continuity, operating on The Goldfish Principle is worse than not doing anything at all; it will actively destroy trust in your brand and also is such an easy thing to discuss on Twitter, as shown later. All you really need to do is understand their individual needs and remember them – this is why treatment plans are so powerful, as they not only provide continuity of care, but also continuity of brand. As Don said "Operating on The Goldfish Principle today doesn't just communicate that you aren't competent enough to run a sound business, it actually broadcasts that you don't care enough about customers even to try to be competent. Don't do it".

HAVE HUMANITY

In Marketing 101, there is talk of the 3P's:

Product – What is our product or service?

Price – What is its cost/value proposition?

Promotion – How are you going to sell it?

All good stuff, but the 3P's weren't enough so there are now seven P's (I'm not going to detail them; if you're interested Google the 7P's of the Marketing Mix). Following this will really help you to get the elements of your business in order, but it doesn't really capture this exciting Post PC era that we are now in.

We need to add the 3H's:

Humans online – How do we support our customers online and through social media?

Humans offline – How do we support our customers when we speak to them?

Humans in your business – How do we support our employees and partners?

Notice here the key word I use is *support*, not *sell* – give and you shall receive. There is an increasing trend of people using Twitter to call out poor service, and you cannot ignore the human element.

Hassan Syed, disgruntled British Airways passenger, spent £1,000 on turning a complaint into a Twitter advert that went viral, slamming BA for losing his luggage.

It trended because it was new and quite funny, and news stories referencing this in articles were also shared, generating more coverage. Mashable attracted 10,000 shares of its article, so think about what kind of online experience you want your customers to have.

The goal of speaking to your customers is clearly to get them into the clinic for a consultation, and a great example of "Offline Customer Experiences" (please forgive me, I have just created marketing jargon) is the Personal Stylist Programme at Nordstrom, a US department store.

My mum LOVES shopping, and I was in a Nordstrom Houston with her for what seemed like three days (thanks for that, Mum), while she had a personal stylist appointment. The Nordstrom Programme is a combination of stylist, fashion buyer, sales, and counselling. It's a free service and the stylist/counsellor gets commission on the sales, but what struck me about it was that it wasn't a huge sell – in fact, that day my mother didn't buy much – but that the strength of the relationship between them was incredible! They were like friends, and my mother now judges every shop by this standard, and expects warmth, empathy and time from all of her interactions with servers.

Go to a Nordstrom and check it out.

If you can't make it to the US, another example is the Apple Genius Bar. Yes, I know I love Apple, but PC World have tried to ape it with the Geek Squad, and it's not quite worked. Why? Because you might think I'm a geek, but I think I'm cool.

BE EASY TO DEAL WITH

The final thought is a simple one – just be easy to talk to. This is very easily said but in practice quite a challenge, especially if you have a large customer base. However, I will use three personal examples to illustrate this point.

Taking my cue from Hassan Syed, I tweeted Vodafone Customer Services after waiting for 20 minutes on hold before being accidentally cut off.

Now how did I feel? As you would – ignored, annoyed, treated with offhand contempt. I did email and two days later received a reply, and, as of time of writing, it has been sorted, but the damage has been done – I no longer trust Vodafone as the right fit for my business.

Is this The Goldfish Principle? Yes.

Is this supporting a customer online? Sort of.

Is this being easy to deal with? No.

Another example is Lego. The Danish toy company is now only behind Mattel as the world's biggest toy manufacturer. Every now and again they get it wrong and there is a missing or deformed brick in the latest expensive Star Wars Lego kit you're being forced to build.

Getting a replacement is easy; there's a no-questions-asked policy on missing bits (and, before you say it, clearly a no-questions-asked returns policy on a medical treatment is not workable, but you get my point).

Ikea, on the other hand, try getting a replacement sent to you if there is a piece missing from a pack, as there is no policy at all on missing components, but definitely a policy of self-righteousness.

By the way, if you haven't completed the Business Growth Score-card, right now is a great time to do that. It's a fantastic tool to help identify how easy you are to do business with, and obviously jumping into the Aesthetic Entrepreneurs programmes is the best way of improving your scores.

So, is customer experience the way forward, or is it just a new way of packaging quality customer service?

Let me know, just leave a message on my voicemail.

I bet you're humming "just keep swimming" all day.

> *"Now, when we fought, you had that eye of the tiger, man; the edge! And now you gotta get it back, and the way to get it back is to go back to the beginning."*

APOLLO CREED – ROCKY III (1982)

MISTAKE NUMBER 5 – TRYING TO SKIP THE STRUGGLE

Aesthetic Entrepreneurs is an overnight success, 15 years in the making. It's hundreds of different threads, notes and ideas all finally getting airtime. It's me finally being me, and the lessons learnt from working on some pretty high-level stuff. Some of these concepts I started developing pre-pandemic all started to connect in my mind. In the third part of this book, you are going to benefit from this experience and connections with some end-to-end processes that will help you take a total stranger to a client. Provided that you do it consistently, it is highly effective and actually quite fun and quite rewarding. How do I know? Because you are reading this book and you're part of the story, you're part of my Rocky montage! I am a big fan of the Rocky movies; they're a full-on part of my cultural heritage. Having older cousins who were well into boxing, and American middleweights with names like "Marvellous" Marvin Hagler, Thomas "The Hitman" Hearns and "Sugar Ray" Leonard were like superheroes. In this time in the early- to mid-80s, Sylvester Stallone and the Rocky films were at their peak.

It's actually on my bucket list to hobble up the Rocky Steps in Philadelphia. I watch the movies at least once a year, and during this year's Rocky marathon it really dawned on me that Rocky is a terrible boxer. If the objective of boxing is to be hit hard many, many times then Rocky has it nailed. Also, they all have exactly the same plot. The plot to Rocky is pretty much as follows:

- Rocky is our hero, and is a loser

- Faced with adversity or hardship, our hero is given a lucky shot at the title

- He finds a mentor

- Rocky works really hard through the montage sequence to almost triumph against the odds

The plot to Rocky II is pretty much the same:

- Rocky is our hero, and is a loser

- Faced with adversity or hardship, our hero is given another shot at the title Rocky works really hard through the montage sequence to triumph against the odds

Rocky III is a tiny bit different:

- Rocky is our hero, and is not a loser anymore

- A baddie comes along and makes him a loser again, and kills his friend/mentor

- Faced with adversity or hardship, our hero is given another shot at the title Rocky goes back to basics and works really hard through the montage sequence to triumph against the odds, with a rock soundtrack

Rocky IV is a bit different to Rocky III:

- Rocky is our hero, and is not a loser anymore because he knows James Brown

- A baddie comes along and makes him a loser again, and kills his friend/mentor

- Faced with adversity or hardship, our hero is given another shot at the title

- Rocky goes back to basics and works really hard through the montage sequence to triumph against the odds, only this time in Russia, and ends the Cold War

I could go on... but I won't because Rocky V is rubbish, but the point is that everyone knows this and continues to watch them.

A last-minute call from No.1 Son, "Dad, let's go and see Creed 2." It's a Sunday, there is nothing on TV, why not? Creed II is pretty much Rocky II, III and IV in the same film. I knew what was going to happen after 10 minutes.

But it didn't bother me. Why? Because I love stories about the hero's journey.

Because we live this same story in our lives, it gives us hope. Rocky cannot triumph over adversity without the adversity.

He cannot have a montage to build himself up if he's not been broken down, and what's the point of having a killer rock soundtrack without the montage?

So many I speak to ask me to try to help them skip to the end of the hero's journey, to help them be heroes without the adversity or montage.

If we do this, look how thin the story becomes:

Rocky is our hero, and is a loser

He triumphs against the odds

Boring. All the interesting bits are gone. You need this montage sequence in order to grow, and it's also the part of the story that everyone is interested in. So stop trying to skip the struggle, stop trying to avoid the adversity.

Know it's coming, embrace it, learn from it, create your montage and give it your best shot. Why does everyone love a Rocky film? It's because they are programmed to.

Create your own hero's journey, and share it.

"It all boils down to today, for you seniors, this marks the culmination of the past four years."

"Culmination."

COACH MARSHALL AND ASSISTANT LACROSSE COACH – AMERICAN PIE (1999)

MISTAKE NUMBER 6 – STARTING TOO BIG

I want you to think about this: there is no honour in minimising yourself.

My entrepreneurial career has been a series of steps. The first was taking the big step to go it alone, and writing this book is the culmination of that phase, that leg of the journey where a lot of the mistakes have been made, and where I've learnt some very valuable lessons and my theories and lessons were created, structured and formalised. One thing I can never be accused of is not think-

---

"You need to remember one thing though – you need to think big, but start small."

ing big enough. If you set yourself on a goal to be the best in the business, in your region, imagine if you miss that target and you become the best in your town. Is that enough for you?

What about changing the world?

The challenge that we as entrepreneurs I think find the hardest, is that we are visionary, we are future thinkers, we are not the detail, that comes later. The biggest lesson I've learnt in the last five years has been to ask, "who is going to buy this and what problem is it solving?" The need to create is in my DNA, I cannot resist the urge that when I see something I can fix, I have to have a go. I hope by the time I get to book number three that changing the world is something that we've achieved, because that's my big hairy ass goal. I've mellowed a bit and have come to terms with not being able to change an entire global industry. I do want to change the world, but I'm going to change it by making my little piece of it better, with a ruthless focus.

You need to remember one thing though – you need to think big, but start small.

I watched an interview with Spike Lee and he summed this up really well for me in that when young film makers would come to him with a script it was often an amazing story. It would go from one place to another, car chases and shoot outs and all these wonderful imaginative things, but it lacked depth.

The reason for this is because the first thing you have to be able to do in his view is write a monologue. One person, speaking to a camera, and make that interesting, make that engaging.

Then, a conversation.

Then, you could film a room full of people, the same process, and then a scene at a block, or a corner, then a street, then a block, then a suburb, then a city.

Because if you can't make a monologue interesting, you will not make a city interesting.

A story that many consider Lee's greatest work, *Do the Right Thing*, takes place on a single day in Brooklyn. It also takes place on a single block.

It is a small story unique to certain neighbourhoods in New York City, until at the end of the film, when suddenly it isn't.

We quickly realise that Lee has been building universal themes and characters all along, as the story climaxes in an explosive ending that is anything but small.

Great stories don't depend on big budgets, special effects, and name stars – they depend on emotion.

When a storyteller can produce deep feelings in her or his audience, the effect surpasses anything. So, what is your story going to be?

Another way to look at my recent adventures is that it was a one-year training course in how to run a global operation, pitching, dealing with investors, dealing with lawyers, dealing with bankers, dealing with techies and realising that while I share the belief in the technology, I don't share the love of technology. I've got good customers, great clients and the ones who are implementing, the ones who are seeing real, real change in their businesses, that's my calling. Passing on what I have learned and helping others achieve their goals. It's what I'm good at. I'm very good at it, and saying that is not arrogant, saying that is belief, because if I don't believe in my abilities, how am I going to help you to believe in yours?

Perception is reality, and I do deal with a lot of people who are struggling badly and don't know where to turn. Once we address that underlying fear and lack of belief they get great results, and it's such a thrill when we see that the business is stable, making money and we have a happy human being. They've got new purpose, new vision, new engagement and a better understanding of the problem that they're solving and the people that they're solving it for.

And they are thinking bigger!

BEING BATMAN

In 1936, two Action Comics writers, Joe Shuster and Jerry Siegel, created a modern-day Hercules, a character who was all powerful – Superman. What a home run! As a major distraction in depression era America, Superman became a hugely popular character, and yet this yielded a big problem – how to follow him up.

An artist called Bob Kane and a young writer called Bill Finger had an interesting solution. They took Superman and mirrored him. Where Superman was light, they needed darkness. Superman was an alien, they needed a human. Superman had infinite powers, they needed no superpowers at all. Superman was honest and truthful, they needed a vigilante. Superman was the American dream, they needed the American truth. What comic character is dark, human, has no superpowers, is a vigilante and has a big dose of realism?

The Batman, one of the most recognisable comic characters in history, created simply by taking the opposite view of Superman.

So, if we take this logic and apply it to our Six Mistakes, flipping them 180 degrees, the secret to greatness is revealed.

MISTAKE NUMBER 1 – Not being authentic

MISTAKE NUMBER 2 – Telling the wrong stories

MISTAKE NUMBER 3 – Not enough understanding of the client's problem

MISTAKE NUMBER 4 – Not creating an experience

MISTAKE NUMBER 5 – Trying to skip the struggle

MISTAKE NUMBER 6 – Starting too big

So, discover your inner Batman and take control of your business – the only thing that really matters is you.

PART 3

HOW DO YOU
WANT TO
GET THERE?

*"Sometimes you eat the bear and,
well, sometimes he eats you."*

THE STRANGER — THE BIG LEBOWSKI (1999)

TAKE RESPONSIBILITY

"**O**wn your shit," Warrant Officer Hussey once said to me. "Own your shit, young man, and earn your pay." Once again, good advice from the Royal Navy, and it's something that I've actually always carried through. I never make excuses for myself or for my actions. In fact, sometimes I'm a little too honest. I remember when I was a kid, about 13 or 14, and me and a mate were walking past a building site, and one of the builders shouted something racially offensive at us. It was Reading in the mid-80s and it kind of just happened, pretty frequently.

As I was back then, I just kind of brushed it off, but my mate wasn't quite so accommodating about being called a "Coon" and he picked up half a brick and lobbed it as hard as he could at this builder. It missed the builder but went through one of the glass windows of the house they were building.

So we legged it down the street (in the mid-1980s era of hip-hop, trying to run in Adidas trainers with no laces was quite hard). We ran around the corner and straight into a copper. Two black youths running away from something, 1980s policing, and a pissed off racist builder. It really wasn't looking good for us.

"Why are you two in such a hurry?" asked the policeman.

"Because there is a bloke chasing us with a piece of wood," I said, retrieving my left trainer from the middle of the road.

The builder comes around the corner. "Who was it? Which one of you little **** was it who threw the brick?" he demanded.

At this point, I was expecting my mate to confess, but he stayed very quiet, went weak at the knees, and then started crying. I thought, fuck it, there's no way he's gonna handle whatever punishment is about to be meted out to him. Mine will probably be altogether less severe and I'm probably a bit more able to take it.

So I fessed up. "Yeah, it was me."

The police officer then starts ripping into me. I managed to get a couple of words in, about the builder calling us Coons as we walked past. "Is this true?" he asked, and the builder looked a bit sheepish.

The copper said, "Well, you've been a bit stupid all round. On your way."

We walked off, and my mate was still very quiet. "Well, you can thank me any time you want," I said.

"As an entrepreneur you must take responsibility for your own life, your own business."

My mate said, "No one asked you to do it."

Our friendship pretty much ended right there and then if I'm honest. I don't mind taking flak for people, but I do expect to be recognised. However, that's what I've always done. I like to stand up for people, fight for the underdog, be protective and help people.

I've never been afraid to own my shit, and it's just got me into trouble a few times, especially in the corporate world. In the Royal Navy, you've all got each other's back, and it's the same on the rugby pitch. In the corporate world, I found that very few people have your back, and people are playing their own game. I was never particularly bothered with office politics and rather naive when it came to that kind of thing. Very, very few take responsibility.

The reason is they don't have to, they can just get another job, but as an entrepreneur you must take responsibility for your own life, your own business. At the end of the day, this entrepreneurial journey that you have embarked on, or you're planning to embark on, is really hard, and there will be points where the world is against you, your back's to the wall and you have to make a decision whether or not you're going to let it beat you or come out swinging.

Sometimes you eat the bear and, well, sometimes he eats you. Either way, you've got to make the decision as to what you're going to do, and 9 times out of 10, the shit that you're in can be directly related to a stupid decision that you made maybe six months ago. It might not be totally your fault, and it's probably not fair, but no one, and I mean no one, is coming to bail you out other than you.

You can get all the advice, all the guidance, read all the books, and listen to all the gurus, but you have to put in the work, and not everyone wants to do that. This is the big difference between the people I coach and mentor and the people I don't:

Team RCS own their shit. It's a fundamental requirement of working with me, and so I've built a team around me that have shared values. Sometimes things have gone wrong due to things outside your control, and, yes, you have the right to recourse. Where an advisor you have hired is useless and delivered rubbish work, that happens, and when that can be traced right back down to poor workmanship, then you have a right to be pissed off.

But did you really do your due diligence properly?

Did you ask for references?

Did you trial?

No?

Then it's your fault. Own it.

You have to take the responsibility of dealing with your customers, you have to take the responsibility for dealing with your suppliers and executing the plan. It's good to have a mentor or a coach to help you create the plan, spot the potential grenades, and see some of the angles, but you have to own it. Owning it gives you power, and no one out there has the right to make you feel any less worthy than you deserve to feel. When your tail is in the air, and your confidence is high, you can achieve anything. But if your head is down, your tail is low and your mind is full of negativity, it's incredibly difficult to get anything done. Often, when working with a client, the first job is to get your head up, build some confidence, start forward scanning and get yourself going. You still have to do the work. I'm not picking up the phone for you, or doing the design or planning for you, you still had to "do the do".

With guidance, support and belief you can achieve great things. Humans thrive in a community, and those who can be coached, are willing to act, will listen and are able to act on quite direct feedback will grow faster as entrepreneurs and make more money faster than those who don't.

You are the leader in your business, and you must take responsibility for yourself, for your life, for your business. When my clients sometimes ask, "Is it OK if today you talk to my significant other/ my marketing manager/someone else?"

"No, I want to talk to you because you're my client and this is your journey, not their journey."

Owning your shit is a decision. It is a decision that is made before the beginning of every day, before you pick up the phone to make that challenging phone call, before you write that challenging email, before you have to do the thing that you don't want to do.

You have to suck it up, buttercup, and get used to the fact that you're now in charge of your business. My job is to build your business by inspiring you, the human behind it, but before we do this there are a few home truths that you need to accept, digest and consider.

"If only I knew this before – doing a course in injectables is the easiest part of this whole journey. Part your money with the training company and you get a certificate. The main story starts when you actually realise that it's a business that you have stepped into and not just an injection skill to your portfolio. You need courage, commitment, strategy and a coach to make this journey to become a real entrepreneur."

NISHA MENON, AESTHETIC ENTREPRENEUR

"You can't handle the truth."

COL. NATHAN JESSUP – A FEW GOOD MEN (1992)

THE THREE HOME TRUTHS

So, here are the horrible truths that you don't want to hear. Ready?

TRUTH NUMBER ONE

People really don't care about you, they literally only care about themselves.

As an entrepreneur, you are very proud of your business, and rightly so. You've taken this idea, your solution to a huge problem, have invested your energy, money, time and love into bringing it into fruition. Here it now stands before you, proud with its logo, identity, and its packages, and the truth is no one actually cares.

"People don't want to be sold to, so don't sell to them. Just educate and inform and create messages that resonate with them."

They don't care about what you do, they only care about themselves and what you can do for them. So many people get it wrong in the beginning and you feel the need to tell everybody how difficult this was, and how much hard work you put into creating this, why it is such an amazing idea. Actually, no one really cares. All anyone ever cares about is, what is it going to do for *me*? How is it going to fix *my* problem?

"Thank you very much for investing a million pounds in this solution, but I don't give a shit about that. I want to pay 50 pence for my problem to go away."

People don't buy drill bits, they buy holes in the wall, and to tell me how a drill bit is made would be a waste of time as I couldn't care less. All I care about is putting a hole in my wall so I can feed the wire to my TV through into the other room, thus ridding my eyeline of unsightly technological bits and pieces that interfere with the *Game of Thrones* experience.

That is the reality.

So tell the world how great you are but don't forget to tell them how great your solution is for the problem that they have. Do this from day one and you'll get much faster growth.

TRUTH NUMBER TWO

People don't want to be sold to on social media. They are on social media to look at pictures of cats doing funny things, other people having better lives than them and to distract from their rubbish lives.

Your latest package/offer/deal is the same as everyone else's. They won't just hand their money over to you because you have asked them to. Most people work hard to get paid, why should they hand it over to you? Most people don't even begin to think about this when marketing. You have to be very careful as it's really easy to turn your audience off on social media, even with the best of intentions.

There are many, many high-quality products that are sold online through multi-level marketing. In the US, due to geography and culture, the Multi-Level Marketing (MLM) model is actually quite a respected and common way to buy. In the UK, however, taking part in a multi-level marketing campaign could see you flayed Ramsay Bolton style (that's a GOT reference for anyone who didn't watch it). Over-selling, over-promising and under-delivering has given it a really poor reputation.

I actually use products that I have purchased through multi-level marketing, yet I've always been very reluctant to tell anyone what these products actually are. I am in a position of influence with Aesthetic Entrepreneurs and I do not want to be associated with the negative connotations of multi-level marketing. So what I do is just pass them on to a company and take nothing from it. This means I maintain my impartiality but still allow people to benefit from what I believe to be a good product. The reason that people don't want to be sold to is because it triggers a heightened emotional state of awareness and it comes across as being insincere.

TRUTH NUMBER THREE

We all tend to purchase in the same way.

Here's an example:

I have what is commonly known as a "rugby player's bottom", which means it is incredibly muscular, over-developed and round. It's quite beautiful actually. Combine that with "rugby player's thighs", which are spectacular quadriceps and a wonder to behold. They are truly majestic specimens and should definitely be placed in the "Museum of Beautiful Quads". If there isn't such a thing, someone should invent it.

Why am I telling you this? Well, having such a large bottom means that buying jeans is a bit of a nightmare. So, over time, I have learned there is a particular manufacturer of jeans (Edwin, and his fine Japanese denim) and a particular style that works really well with me and my big bottom, magnificent thighs and museum-worthy calves. Anyway, there is a shop in Brighton that I know stocks these, and their flagship store in London. So when it comes to the time to replace one pair of jeans with another, I know exactly what shop to go to. I know who makes them and I know what size. I make the little trip into Brighton to get them and walk into the shop. Rather than go straight for the jeans, I'll do the little British shopping dance. Which is you go in and look for something that you're not interested in, such as shoes or a tank top, and when someone says, "Can I help you, sir?", despite the fact you do actually need help, you always say, "No". After a few minutes holding up stuff I don't like I will then, silently, go and have a look at the jeans, waiting impatiently for the man who, barely two minutes ago, asked me if I needed any help and I said, "No," to, to come and ask me if I need any help because now I do. I suspect the reason we say, "No," is because there is a deep-seated cultural fear that the dude who owns the shop is going to try and sell me something. I don't want to be sold to, I want to choose to buy.

I want to maintain control of the conversation, and the way I do that is to try and confuse him by not looking at the jeans first. I determine when I make that step. And a good retailer, distributor, salesperson is literally there, when I'm ready to make that step, on hand to help me and guide me through my purchasing decision. That's what should happen in a retail environment, and it is absolutely the same online. In social media, putting out consistent messaging for your target market that resonates with them is the way to make sure that, when they are ready to choose, you are on hand. If someone had created a marketing campaign that said, "Are you a former rugby player with a large bottom, spectacular quadriceps and most triumphant calves?", I'd be like, "Yeah, that's me". Miriam would agree too. If they then said, "Do you struggle buying jeans?", I'd think, "Ooh yes, I do. Definitely. Ooh, what's this?" and if they followed that with, "Would you like a made-to-measure pair of fine Japanese denim jeans?" I'd be like, "Hell, yeah!!" I would fall over in my desperation for more information. I have been sold to, but I am interested, because it's a problem that is solved. The problem is that I don't have to visit the Levi's store and get a pair of spray-on jeans that make me look like Mr Incredible.

By creating a hyper-targeted marketing campaign, it has almost guaranteed that I'm interested and I'm clicking through, along with everyone else who has my problem.

People don't want to be sold to, so don't sell to them. Just educate and inform and create messages that resonate with them. This is a mindset that you MUST adopt if you are to successfully build trust and create a business that is truly unique.

So now you are suitably prepared for the journey ahead, let's get stuck in!

Reminder – You can treat this as a training programme, designed to rebuild your business in the next few months, and work with me, through this book, as a partner.

To help you do this you can find lots of
free information and support here.

"Just the other night I was sleeping under a bridge and now here I am on the grandest ship in the world having champagne with you fine people."

JACK DAWSON — TITANIC (1997)

THE JOURNEY TO SUCCESS

STEP ONE — SET CLEAR GOALS

You might be thinking *goal setting again?*, and I'll let you off that, but one of my observations is that people still often just go through the motions on setting goals, and they are nowhere near developed enough. If you need a refresher, go back and read the earlier chapter on goal setting, as we are going to dig in a level deeper.

You read that chapter, I told you the importance, and did you set your goals?

Did you really set your goals?

Did you use the resources?

Did you listen to Stevie?

You need to, because business is hard, there is no getting away from that fact. So go back and do it. In the earlier chapters you have heard all about the trials and tribulations of your humble narrator over the past few years. What has kept me going through all of this is the Burning Desire and a very understanding and supportive wife. My Burning Desire is to be successful, to help my clients change their lives. I wake up every morning consumed with the desire to help my family achieve their goals, to help Lana, Isaac, Toby, Persie and Amy to become all they can be. To honour the sacrifices of Vernon and Sheila, my grandparents who left Barbados in the 1950s, and Pauline, Miriam and Sid who all helped to raise me. To honour the patience and love of Caroleann, and Andy, Patrick and Inge, my mother and stepfather and father and stepmother; and repay Ian and Margaret, Amy's parents, for the faith and support they have shown in me. But more important than all of this, is to realise my potential. I can't change the whole world, but I can change my little piece of it.

That is my goal. It's strong, and I can feel it in my core. Even as I write this down I can feel the energy that goal gives me. You must have this energy because business is all about managing risk, and I once believed that planning helped to mitigate risk, but actually in reality planning doesn't mitigate anything, it just helps you see the risks more clearly. During my days working in project management, a key lesson I learned was that when faced with a roadblock there are only really ever three things you can do:

1. Do nothing.

2. Do a little.

3. Do a lot.

Once you accept this then decision making becomes far easier and less stressful. The fear we have is in making a bad decision, or choosing a path that is "make or break", when nothing apart from suicide is really a make or break decision. I work with clients to enable them to make a series of decisions that will, over the course of time, lead towards a defined goal. The plan is the framework you create to enable you to take as much risk out of those decisions as possible. You cannot eliminate risk, so stop trying. Everything has a risk, and you can either accept that risk, evaluate the impact and either get on with it or reject the risk and not do it.

Over the years, I've learned to use some really simple tools and tips to help me, and using them gave me massive success, only for me to then stop doing it, which is a daft thing to do really!

You think, oh, this is all brilliant, I don't need to do it anymore. So you stop, and only when you've stopped do you realise actually it's really, really good. Human nature at its finest. From a learned planner, I guarantee that if you implement a plan it will make you money. So harness the goal – it's what you need to drive you, to create the plan that will help you crystallise and achieve that goal, which is step two in the process.

"Your vision and values are the foundation that your sales and marketing is built on. In fact, they are the principles that your entire business is built on."

STEP TWO – HAVE A CLEAR PLAN OF ACTION

On the Business Growth Scorecard, one of the questions I ask you is "Do you have a business plan that I can see *right now?*" The clue to the importance of the question is "right now". At the time of writing, nearly 1,000 people have completed that question, and do you want to guess how many answered "yes"?

Not one.

Not one single person answered "yes".

1,000 people and not a single plan.

When I talk to a new client, or even a potential new client, things generally have just started off, or sometimes they are in the shit. It's rare that I get a call that starts off with "How are you, Rich? Everything is tip-top, let's work together". I'd actually love that. But a lot of the time there is a stressed person on the end of the phone, and they are often totally overwhelmed. The first thing we need to do in this instance is quieten the mind and bring a bit of order to manage the fear, and the way to do that is to create a plan.

One planning strategy that is highly effective was taught to me by my last boss at Allergan, an incredibly talented lady called Heather Hancock. Heather is an incredible digital strategist, leader and mentor with 20 years' experience within the healthcare industry. She has generated BILLIONS in revenue, holds an MBA, a double honours degree in Biochemistry and Chemistry, has two children, one crazy dog and a ginger tomcat. It's amazing how life moves, as in 2010 Heather practically sacked me from my key account manager role. I needed to do more and spread my wings, and it's a testament to her leadership that she saw this. Fast forward to now, and Heather leads the Strategy sessions for our business programmes and gave me this nugget of wisdom. It's so simple, but incredibly effective. You just take all the elements that you need to cover off, all the little things that need to be done, and just dump them on a piece of paper.

She called it the List of Life. To you it might be a brain dump. Whatever you want to call it, just take some time at the beginning of the week, or maybe even on Sunday night, to relax and get everything down on a piece of paper. Once you've done that, pause and do it again. Do this a couple of times and you'll soon squeeze every last little thing out of your head that you've got to get done. It's incredibly cleansing; however, once you have got it all out, you could be faced with a list from hell staring back at you, which isn't going to help your stress levels.

What will help is a process of prioritisation. This is a part of the process I think people really struggle with. I know I did, because often it feels like everything is a priority. Well, truth is it's not, and a great way to establish what is a priority and what isn't is to use an Eisenhower Matrix.

Dwight David "Ike" Eisenhower was an American army general and statesman who served as the 34th president of the United States from 1953 to 1961. During World War II, he was a five-star general in the United States Army and served as supreme commander of the Allied Expeditionary Forces in Europe.

He was responsible for planning and supervising the invasion of North Africa in Operation Torch in 1942–43 and "D-Day", the successful invasion of France and Germany in 1944–45 from the Western Front. The "Eisenhower Matrix" stems from a quote attributed to him which was: "I have two kinds of problems, the urgent and the important. The urgent are not important, and the important are never urgent." Using this method, tasks are evaluated using the criteria important/unimportant and urgent/not urgent, and then placed in according quadrants in an Eisenhower Matrix, also known as an "Eisenhower Box" or "Eisenhower Decision Matrix".

1. Important/Urgent quadrant are DONE FIRST and personally, e.g. crises, deadlines, problems, sales.

2. Important/Not Urgent quadrant are SCHEDULED and are done personally, e.g. relationships, planning, recreation.

3. Unimportant/Urgent quadrant are DELEGATED, e.g. interruptions, meetings, activities.

4. Unimportant/Not Urgent quadrant are ELIMINATED, e.g. time wasters, pleasant activities, trivia, Ozzy Man.

So once you've got your priorities sorted, you can then map out into the matrix. Every Sunday, myself and Amy look at what jobs need doing in the next week and we work out who's doing what. We also look at what projects we have in the pipeline, who is doing what, and what needs to be done. If you do this, it will turbo-charge your productivity. You'll become far more efficient with your time and find yourself doing the right things. Get the right people in the right place doing the right things and you'll get the right result, just as if you get the right people in the right place doing the wrong things, you'll get a result, it just won't be the one that you want.

THINK, PLAN, DO

"Think, plan, do," was the mantra of Sir Clive Woodward, who famously led the England rugby union team to victory in the 2003 World Cup, and it is still a favourite of mine.

What this means in reality is that in order to execute a plan, we must go through a few different phases. However, a major mistake many entrepreneurs seem to make is to dive straight in at the deep end without going through a process to find out what is actually in the deep end. It could be a treasure chest filled with gold, or it could be a massive great white shark. I've done this a few times myself. When I have my latest fantastic idea that will revolutionise the world, I must create it now. I did exactly this with iConsult, and if I had my time again, I would follow a clear process to enable me to map out the journey, test against the market and fully understand what I am letting myself in for. This needs to be balanced, however, against the sheer cost, complexity and time involved in designing, building and marketing. The process I now follow can help you to avoid making the same mistakes as me. You can apply this to almost anything, from evaluating whether or not to buy a piece of capital equipment through to the effectiveness of a marketing campaign. The foundation of any process that requires decision making is to understand the objective. What exactly are you trying to achieve? This is obviously a huge question, and it has many layers of complexity in the answer. If we applied it to a capital equipment purchase, one of the objectives would be to increase revenue. But that is not specific enough. We need to drill down to understand the objective, assess whether or not we have the resources available to achieve it, make sure that we have the buy-in from our team or significant other, look at how we can implement the changes, and then know how we can test it and make sure the outcome is working.

OBJECTIVE > RESOURCE > BUY-IN > IMPLEMENTATION > TEST = ORBIT

The ORBIT process gets you thinking about your ideas and looking for the safe place to land them. Having a clear objective is fundamental. Remember, people often fail to achieve a goal not through lack of effort, but because the goal is wrong in the first place.

So make sure you test your goal against the methodology described in the "Goal Setting" chapter. If it doesn't stand up, don't do it.

Resource is something which is often hugely overestimated, especially around the desire to get new patients or implement a plan. It is easy to overestimate what we as individuals can achieve in a month while totally underestimating what a team can achieve in a year. I've asked aesthetic practitioners in the past, "If I could give you one wish for your business, what would it be?" The majority of them answer, "More patients". Is that the answer you would give? Don't get me wrong, attracting new customers is a key part of your business. So, wish granted. In one minute, your phone is going to start to ring with 1,000 new patients eager to come to see you. Because that's what you wanted, right? More patients?

What resources will you need to service 1,000 new enquiries? Can you really handle that many? Could you cope with the influx of new business? Unless you have the right processes in place, your wish could become a nightmare.

In this industry, your resources are effectively time, money and knowledge, and you need all three in place. So, if you launch a mega successful new offer, make sure you can cope with the demand. If you knew you had 1,000 new clients coming, you could prepare resources for them, employing a call handling service, and get additional help to manage the treatments. It's all about having your key assets in place before you begin. If you want to build a strong bucket rather than a leaky sieve, you must have a rock-solid client pathway.

Buy-in is an interesting concept, and relatively rare in the aesthetic and beauty market because it's dominated by owner-operated businesses. If you're the boss, why do you need to get buy-in?

The reason you need to get buy-in is it will stop you from making some godawful decisions. As the head of your own business, sometimes you can't see the wood for the trees, especially if the decision is difficult or emotionally charged, so why not bounce it off someone? This is where the Aesthetic Entrepreneurs community is so valuable; you're a boutique or sole practitioner, ask your partner, friend – anyone who will give you an objective answer. If it comes back positive, then move to the next step, but listen to the feedback – it's a gift. Assuming everything is positive, you now need to think about how you are actually going to make it work. For me, implementation is the absolute key to success – "Excellence in execution", as a former boss used to say, and he was right. Even if you have a flawed objective, limited resource and no buy-in, execute a plan well and you will get a result – just not the one you are expecting.

I often set up a post on Facebook to test a new product idea. I had a clear objective, the resources to hand, buy-in from my team and I knew what my goal was, so I tagged ninety people and posted it. I achieved my goal of having ten prospects engage with the trial, but I was also unfriended by ten people who resented being tagged. The next time I had an idea to test, I briefed our Content Ninja team who deal with all our social media and content and handed the implementation over to them. Guess what happened? Yep, I got double the response and no one unfriended me, because they know what they are doing. Implementation doesn't mean doing it yourself; it means getting the right people in the right places, doing the right things to get the right results.

The final part of the ORBIT process is to test/review the outcome. The purpose of the test is to answer one very simple question: "How do I know this has worked?" As the old saying goes, "If you don't know where you're going, any road will take you there", so choose an outcome that is linked to your objective.

If you underpin your sales and marketing plans with the ORBIT framework, your decision making will become significantly more successful.

STEP THREE – DEFINE YOUR CULTURE

There is one thing that continues to astonish me whenever I deal with a client – the lack of strategic planning that they employ in the business. Once you have defined your plan, and we know what we want to achieve and why we want to achieve it, it's time for the part of the process that no one seems to actually want to do.

DEFINE WHO THEY ARE, WHAT THEY STAND FOR AND WHO THEY SERVE.

Many have been in business for a long time but have done very little, if any, work on identifying who it is they are actually serving. Well, it's time to fix all that, because it's of real importance that you do. I've had it drummed into me from very, very early in my commercial career, be it in sales or marketing, that you must know who it is that you're selling to.

You need to know what motivates them, what drives them, the challenges they face. Not just on a superficial level either, as if we agree that sales is simply problem solving, then you need to have a deep understanding of the problem. The deeper the understanding, the more resonance you'll generate, the more resonance, the more you'll connect, the more you connect, the deeper the trust, the deeper the trust, the stronger the relationship and the more you'll sell without having to sell. But before we can even contemplate the consumer, we MUST use our goals and our plan to define our own vision and values and tell YOUR story.

Your vision is a statement of purpose – "We do this, for these people, by doing this."

Our vision?

TO BUILD SUCCESSFUL AESTHETIC BUSINESSES BY INSPIRING THE PEOPLE BEHIND THEM

Your values are how you achieve that purpose.

Our values?

BE PROGRESSIVE – CREATE AND INVEST IN PEOPLE AND IDEAS

BE POWERFUL – GENERATE A POSITIVE IMPACT

BE PRINCIPLED – STAND FOR SOMETHING MEANINGFUL

Your vision and values are the foundation that your sales and marketing is built on. In fact, they are the principles that your entire business is built on. By defining our vision, I identified that I wanted to work with people, and create a human-to-human business. By defining our values, we now have a framework to evaluate whether or not a course of action is in keeping with our brand messages.

IS IT PROGRESSIVE? WILL IT DRIVE US AND OUR CLIENTS FORWARD?

IS IT POWERFUL? WILL IT STAND OUT AND MAKE AN IMPACT?

IS IT PRINCIPLED? WILL IT STAND FOR SOMETHING?

If I think of "the Consumer" and imagine it as a person, I visualise a big, spoilt teenager, demanding everything and giving no thought to the consequences. The reality is that the consumer gets what it wants every time, and it is this that has led to a split in the UK Medical Aesthetic sector. There is a demand from the consumer to treat injectables as lifestyle products and services.

The medical community would like to see them kept as medical, and you don't need to be a genius to work out who will win. It's always the one with the money that calls the tune and it is commercially attractive to align injectables with the consumer. This is why the safety messages bounce off; the consumer does NOT consider injectables to be medical. In their mind Botox has more in common with a Mulberry bag than a drug. They want to have them delivered to THEM where THEY want to be, and they ALWAYS get what they want.

When we first have a clarity call, the first thing I will ask you is "Do you know who your target customer is?" Most of the time I'll get some vague response, which generally ends up as "no". If you don't know who your target client is, you are marketing totally blind. Your messages will be completely ineffective and you will not connect at all with anyone; you are simply wasting your time and money. I was once told that you need to know your customer so well you can predict what colour pants they will wear on Sunday. If you can get to that level, you can become hyper targeted. It's time to understand about customer avatars. It's crucially important that you do this, and not enough work is being done to identify who you're actually selling to, and what you can do for them. There are lots of great resources on the internet for customer avatars or buyer personas, and I've taken the best bits from my favourite ones to create the one to rule them all, and I'm going to share it with you now.

This exercise will make you money, save you time, make you better looking, and able to leap buildings in a single bound. No activity you do will help you to resonate more with your target market than this. It will save you money because all you need to do once you've completed it is pump it into Facebook and create your lookalike audience, and your ads will instantly be more effective. I give you my you-can't-bend-it, gold-star, iron- clad, locked-in, super-duper guarantee. It's detailed, so I'm going to break it down into different stages.

Before we get stuck into this, I need you to quieten your mind, so find somewhere you can just close your eyes, relax and visualise. I need you to visualise your ideal client, while we go through a series of questions, and you need to be as specific as possible.

A good tip here is to have someone else ask you the questions and you record your answers using Rev or an audio app.

We need to create a full story for your client. If you have a client like your ideal already, that's fantastic, just describe them. If you don't, just copy this model. This is a meaty topic, so take your time and use the resources in the MAETRIX to support you through this.

EXERCISE: AVATAR

BACKGROUND

First things first, what is their name?

Are they male or female?

How old are they?

Are they married? Who too? How long for?

Do they have kids?

How many? How old?

DEMOGRAPHIC

What do they do for a living?

How much do they earn?

What car do they drive?

KEY IDENTIFIERS

What social media network are they normally on?

What is their communication style? Are they direct/reserved?

Are they an extrovert or an introvert?

GOALS

What do they want to achieve?

PROBLEMS

What is stopping them from achieving those goals?

What is the problem they have?

Don't just immediately jump to solving; think, and don't think superficially about it, because you can guarantee it's not just about their skin.

HOW DO THEY FEEL?

Are they under pressure at work?

Are they having to compete against other people in the job?

Are they job hunting themselves?

Dig deeper.

WHAT CAN WE DO?

How can you help them to achieve their goals?

Once you have really dug into the problem, ask yourself, how can I help them to solve those problems?

You need to think about it from an emotional perspective because that is where the real pay-off is. It's not about making their skin more shiny. It's changing the way they feel about themselves.

REAL QUOTES

How do your clients describe the problem?

What words do they use?

Get some exact quotes, ask them.

COMMON OBJECTIONS

Why don't they want what you are selling?

MARKETING MESSAGES

How do you describe your solution to those problems?

This is what is commonly called your "Elevator Pitch".

Position that solution to the problem to your ideal client, because only by understanding problems can you create solutions for them, and it's this little part here that people stop doing and they don't focus on problem solving.

How do they feel?

Are they tired, and is that fatigue manifesting itself in their personal appearance?

One of the keys to this is the more you understand your clients, the more you understand how you can help them. And then you just craft your marketing messages around that and around your solution to that problem.

This is a process that I go through in my own business as well.

We have four customer avatars. I have The Kelly, The Stevie, The Nicci and The Hayley.

Each one of these avatars has different and unique challenges. They are often someone who's coming into aesthetics for the first time, someone a bit further down the road, an established clinic and industry supplier. In this book, we are focusing on the challenges that The Kelly and The Stevie have, but don't worry, there is another book in the wings that will help The Niccis and The Hayleys!

So take some time with this. If you need some help you might want to consider the Aesthetic Entrepreneurs programme. People buy from people like them. People have people they trust and like attracts like. So that's why we talk an awful lot about resonant marketing, but also authenticity and being yourself because ultimately the more you do that, the happier you'll be. You will attract people who share your values, share your belief systems, and your business will run much, much smoother.

STEP FOUR – CREATE A COMMUNITY

Authenticity is a word that is becoming increasingly used in the marketing world and simply for me it means just being yourself. People know when someone is being disingenuous, it sticks out a mile. Authenticity means allowing your personality to shine through in your marketing and to connect your beliefs with your ideal client.

For example, veganism is very much on trend in the aesthetics world. If you are claiming that you're vegan friendly, but you are doing it to be on trend and couldn't actually care less about veganism, you will not be able to sustain that messaging and will appear totally inauthentic to that audience. However, dissonance isn't a bad thing.

We cannot be all things to all people, yet many try to do exactly that when they advertise or market their business. Being all things to all people means you are being nothing to no one, and it's this lack of bravery that will hamper your business growth.

The final benefit of resonance is that you will attract partnerships, and this is a fantastic opportunity that many miss. Once you have identified your ideal client, it's relatively easy to then identify other businesses that serve them. It doesn't need to be the obvious contenders either. One of my clients partnered with the local Audi dealership and ran an event. If they sell to your avatar, they are connected. So think out of the box, be creative, be authentic, be bold, be brave, don't be boring.

Be yourselves!! There are some great examples of resonant marketing, and one of the best in the last couple of years has been the Nike 30th anniversary "Just do it" campaign with the former San Francisco 49ers quarterback, Colin Kaepernick. In the 49ers third preseason game of the 2016 season, Kaepernick was noticed sitting down during the playing of "The Star-Spangled Banner" as opposed to the tradition of standing during the national anthem. During a post-game interview, he explained his position, stating, "I am not going to stand up to show pride in a flag for a country that oppresses black people and people of colour. To me, this is bigger than football and it would be selfish on my part to look the other way. There are bodies in the street and people getting paid leave and getting away with murder".

Kaepernick was referencing a series of African-American deaths caused by US police that led to the Black Lives Matter movement. Kaepernick later opted to kneel during the US national anthem rather than sit and explained his decision to switch was an attempt to show more respect to former and current US military members while still protesting during the anthem after having a conversation with former NFL player and US military veteran, Nate Boyer.

KAEPERNICK WENT ON TO KNEEL DURING THE ANTHEM PRIOR TO EVERY 49ERS GAME THAT SEASON.

Regardless of your point of view on this subject, Nike has a history of doing incredibly well timed and politically divisive marketing campaigns that all come from a place of authenticity. It's easy to get it wrong, but the simple fact about authenticity is it's about belief. I don't actually believe that Nike is into politics, I believe that it loves marketing and selling gear. Nike spends millions on research every year. So, choosing Kaepernick to be the face of the campaign was a very calculated decision. The company was built on rebellion and bucking the system and Kaepernick falls right in line with that. Michael Jordan and Steve Prefontaine were Nike's cornerstone athletes, and both bucked the system. Prefontaine was an eccentric runner who challenged the established norms (if you don't know who he is in the UK, he's the athlete that the 118 adverts are based on).

Nike took a major chance on a black athlete as their star in the 80s, the Nike "Air Jordans" were banned by the NBA, but he continued to wear them, with Nike allegedly paying the $5,000 per game fine every time. When the Nike advert hit the US, it was challenging, aggressive, memorable, meme worthy, shareable and emotive. It really pushed buttons and it challenged Nike customers. People burned Nike shoes, Nike got airtime; people cut the swoosh out of their socks, Nike got airtime; the President was appalled, Nike got airtime. Under Armour had Dwayne "The Rock" Johnson, Nike now had civil rights. Now, if you're burning your Nike shoes, then you weren't really a Nike customer. They didn't want you, they weren't bothered, because Nike knows the value of community and creating a tribe.

By shaking things and resonating with those who identified with Black Lives Matter and Colin Kaepernick, both in the US and overseas, they gained a more engaged, active follower base and instantly became relevant again.

NOTHING EVER COMES FROM BEING BORING, FROM JUST TOEING THE LINE.

STAND FOR SOMETHING. I stand for the entrepreneur. I stand for those who are interested in business. I don't talk about the clinical aspects of it. Maybe that was seen as controversial in my forum, the fact that I delete clinical comments, but the reason it's controversial is because those people did not share my belief systems or my values enough to respect my views, respect my wishes and the wishes of my clients that we wanted to have a forum that was uncluttered by clinical discussion. The reason we don't have clinical discussion is because that's where your comfort zone lies. You know far more than me about your job. You're supposed to. I know far more than you about mine. And that's right, because I'm supposed to. So if I allowed you to talk about your job, that's what you would do. You talk about why you're the best in the world at what you do. I'm talking about how to tell the rest of the world that you're the best in the world at what you do. And we can't do that if all you're talking about are syringe sizes. So that is why we don't do it. That decision split the deck and meant that some people did not want to engage with our community.

Now, the no dickhead rule is there in place to filter out those who do not belong in our tribe. And it's not being exclusive. It's being inclusive, but inclusive of the right people. The messaging, the way I have the Facebook Lives, the general feeling and vibe in the group and the way that we conduct ourselves, is designed specifically to attract people who listen to what I've got to say, who respect the point of view of others and are driven to take their business to the next level. And it's highly effective. But I can only do this because I know the problems that my clients have and I really, really want to help them solve those problems.

You cannot fake authenticity, because when you try it blows up in your face.

STEP FIVE – MAXIMISE OPPORTUNITIES

One of the most common questions I'm asked is "Rich, what's the best way to get new clients?" My response is always the same: create a Facebook group, get your clients in there and do Facebook Lives.

The response to this is often, "what's the next best way?" However, if you've had the pleasure of being part of the Aesthetic Entrepreneurs Facebook group, you'll have been listening to me banging on quite a lot about a different kind of 'Live' that is an incredibly powerful tool in your marketing toolkit if you use it properly. Of course, I mean Facebook Live – I've been banging on about it enough!! We have been using this in our own group for a while now, and I'd like to share with you a little bit about what I've learned from doing them. Now, at the time it was kind of something I'd dabbled in a little bit but I hadn't really explored it in any great detail. Frankly, it scared the living piss out of me. Even a ridiculous personality type like mine, if you liberally sprinkle with beer, I'm all over this, but actually sometimes I'm quite reserved. I was just coming from a place of fear, "Who is really interested in what I have to say?"

I was a little bit reticent about how to do it and I remember my first one. There were about 30 people in our fledgling Aesthetic Entrepreneurs community at that point. I went live at the bottom of my garden. It was quite nerve-wracking, but in the end I got into the flow. As long as I had a point, a topic and a structure, I was OK. What I didn't realise was the impact that that would have on me and my business. Once people started listening to me and I'd started getting engagement, I realised, I finally realised, that I had something to say, that people were listening, implementing it and getting success.

There is nothing that beats the confidence gained from success, and I began to open up and grab all the opportunities that were there in front of me. You have bought this book because you are interested in what I had to say, and all of this created the monster that you have before you. I do Facebook Lives a couple of times each week in two different groups, and people get great enjoyment and engagement from being part of that community. They invite their friends into the community because they all get value from it as well.

It's been fantastic fun and a great place to be. We realised that the best time to do them was in the evening and I think some people do find it quite strange that I basically get paid to talk to people through a computer, and my sons get mighty upset when I boot them off *Fortnite*. I created the group, you created the community, and the community generates the engagement and relationship.

This is nothing that you cannot do for your business. You can use these tools. I really encourage you to grow a pair and start doing things like Facebook Live. This will give you a clear differentiation in your marketplace and it'll help you grow your business. If I told you you'd get £300 for every Live you did, would you? Of course you would, and that is exactly what happens to some of my clients. After clarity, understanding your client, knowing what your core is and what your big message is, we need to start looking at how to make you visible. Facebook Lives will help, but real visibility comes from having a bit more of a detailed plan.

If you want to create more conversations, build more relationships and convert them to sales then visibility is absolutely key to your business. I often think of Facebook as a digital country with over two billion residents and its own political system that did, at times, operate outside of what would commonly be called «ethical" boundaries. Mark Zuckerberg himself has been accused of creating a kind of dictatorship and was asked to address US Congress and clarify certain aspects of how Facebook worked. Out of this controversy, one thing became very clear – Facebook needed to change. Throughout 2018 they made tweaks and changes to the algorithm that governs what content we see when we use the platform. They also spent millions on a global advertising campaign to help reinforce and remind us that social media, at its core, is about engaging with a community. By harnessing that philosophy, we can actually work with the algorithm to create better conversations, build stronger relationships and, ultimately, convert those relationships to sales. Facebook loves live videos. If you are really interested in how Facebook works (if you are spending a bucket load on paid ads, I would advise it), here is a really good blog *https://blog.bufferapp.com/facebook-algorithm*. But, if you can't be bothered, here is the headline:

It's all about giving you meaningful content. That's the key, and you need to remember this. Facebook is going to show you what it thinks you want to see, not what advertisers, publishers or marketers want you to see. This is why there has been a drop in reach and why my old school friends from Reading have been suddenly thrust into my Facebook feed.

In addition to this, the Facebook team has been tracking the change in behaviour and how content is being used and have seen that videos have higher levels of engagement than text. So, in line with their meaningful content strategy, Facebook has decided to show you more videos. Over time, they have also learned that certain actions people take while watching a video, such as choosing to turn on sound or making the video full screen, are good signs they wanted to see that video, even if they didn't choose to like it

The Facebook Live platform was launched in 2015, but the first viral hit came in May 2016, when the 37-year-old Texan, Candace Payne, spent four minutes demonstrating a Chewbacca mask in a fit of giggles. It currently has 180 million views on the social network: *https://www.facebook.com/candaceSpayne/videos/10209653193067040/.*

This video, for me, set the precedent for Facebook Live and showed that it's all about authenticity. Facebook Live allows you to see behind-the-scenes; it shows insight; it shows humanity; it's not edited; it's not polished; it's raw. It is the epitome of meaningful content. You can interact with your audience in a way that is just not possible in any other medium. It's not about the numbers, it's about the engagement! Facebook Lives have, on average, six times more engagement than a pre-recorded video and Facebook's algorithm moves it to the top of the news feed. If you want to be seen, this is the way to do it.

This is all about authenticity and engagement, not overly staged, with a Hollywood-level production quality, and showing a different side to you and your business. How you do them will be different to me, so what can you do?

What kind of things can you talk about? All of us love to feel like we have an exclusive look at something that other people don't have access to. So, peel back the curtain on your business process, your decisions, your daily operations and your life. Whatever you feel comfortable sharing (and whatever you don't mind a competitor viewing). Show your customers how you make your "Special Sauce", give them access to a side of your business few have ever seen before.

You can do workshops, training, treatments, staff birthdays – just have some fun! These types of quick tips or daily tips can become a popular social media feature if they're filled with useful information. If you host an event, live-streaming it is a great way to engage with your customers and followers. Chances are you have plenty of followers who want to attend the event but can't afford to. Instead of limiting access, open it by live-streaming aspects of the event. You can also take the best-viewed sessions later and offer them as stand-alone videos. Make it part of your marketing plan.

If you are hosting an event, in the run-up to it do a Facebook Live to announce it. If you're going to host a Facebook Live event, you can announce that too. We have these tools at our disposal, like Facebook, like Instagram, but without a plan they are just tools.

So, do your own Facebook Live. I'm not going to teach you how to use the platform because Facebook does that pretty well on its own page. But what I can do is give you a little structure that enables you to create the process.

So how to structure your Facebook Live? Again, lean into the MAETRIX here, and check out the Facebook Live content, and you will actually see how Kelly progressed, developed and has visibly grown in confidence.

Here's how you can run your broadcast.

The Announcement of your Facebook Live (the pre-launch):

1. Introduce yourself! "Hi, I'm Richard Crawford-Small from the Aesthetic Entrepreneurs and today I'm going to be talking to you about/introducing..."

2. Signal – tell them WHAT you're going to be talking about, "I'm here to announce a very special Date at 8 for Thursday".

3. Entice – tell them WHY you're going to be talking about your chosen topic, "because on Thursday we will be discussing the importance of customer engagement".

4. Promote – tell them WHEN, "we're going to be back here on Thursday, in the Aesthetic Entrepreneurs at 8pm".

5. Thanks and close – remember to engage with your audience. If Karen from accounting has popped on, say "hello". If anyone has asked any questions, answer them.

It really is that simple.

Now, when it comes to doing a longer Facebook Live event, this is the template we follow.

Basically, it's based on the rule of threes.

The introduction is about who you are and what you're going to talk about – the three points. Then you tell them point one, point two, point three. Then you summarise point one, point two, point three, and that's it, job done.

Intro: Who am I?

Story: Why I am going to tell you what I'm going to tell you.

Pause: Welcome the people who are watching, engage, say hi.

Agenda: What I'm going to tell you.

Point one.

Point two.

Point three.

Pause: Welcome the people who are watching, engage, say hi.

Go through point one.

Pause: Welcome the people who are watching, engage, say hi.

Go through point two.

Pause: Welcome the people who are watching, engage, answer questions.

Go through point three.

Pause: Welcome the people who are watching, engage, answer questions.

Summarise all three points – what I have told you.

Call to action: What I want you to do next.

As a final note, here are a few other elements you want to consider.

1. Sound and vision. Make sure you can be seen, but more importantly, make sure you can be heard!

2. Filters are amazing but think about your audience.

3. Be aware of the time lag between what you've said and when people see/hear it.

4. Recap and summarise content at various points.

5. Be aware that it will be watched later.

6. Minimum of 10 minutes.

7. Respond to comments live and give shout-outs.

8. Have someone with you. It can be useful to have another pair of eyes monitoring feedback/questions or any tech issues.

9. Relax and try to enjoy it. It can be fun!

10. Everyone wants you to succeed.

Environments like this are totally amazing for communicating and adding value. They are also something that can be used in your own day-to-day marketing, and you can amplify your reach like crazy through a powerful process called Repurposing.

Kelly likes them too.

"Live videos became king to me, giving people my time, my knowledge and insight starting conversations and in-turn their treatment, skincare journey. What happened next was my business grew and grew." K

STEP SIX – DESIGN THE JOURNEY

Through the years, I have become exposed to many different client journeys and processes, and what has become apparent is that businesses have unconsciously, rather than consciously, created their client journey and don't set clear signposts on what to expect. If you don't set a clear process then you cannot measure its effectiveness, and if you can't measure something, how do you know it works? A good example is Tesco Metro. How many times have you gone in for a pint of milk and come out having spent just under £10? The answer is lots, and it's not an accident, it's designed that way. Millions has been spent on understanding the customer journey, so they know that putting the milk at the furthest possible corner of the store means you have to walk past the Raisin & Biscuit Yorkies and beer. This is annoying, as I love both Raisin & Biscuit Yorkies and Beer.

So what is the secret to an amazing client journey? Simple – you add value!

The Investopedia definition of «Value Added" is "The enhancement a company gives its product or service before offering the product to customers. Value added is used to describe instances where a firm takes a product that may be considered a homogeneous product, with few differences (if any) from that of a competitor, and provides potential customers with a feature or add-on that gives it a greater sense of value".

A less dry way of explaining it is harnessed in a simple sentence – "Create an experience".

Making sense now? Good.

Your client journey needs to achieve three things:

1. Strengthen and build the relationship between you and your client.

2. Build insane levels of trust.

3. Help you to maximise the value of each and every client.

From the moment a client considers having an aesthetic treatment, to the time they're showing off the results of your work to their friends, they need to be actively transitioned through a four-stage process:

- Acquisition (How we attract a new lead)

- Activation (Turning them into a client)

- Consultation (Delivering our solution)

- Retention (Following up)

(By the way – there is a workbook and video to accompany this available on the MAETRIX.) By segmenting the customer journey, you have greater control over each part. Right here is where we really begin to drill down into your current process, reimagining and reinventing it for the 21st century.

The path a client takes to arrive in your clinic is not a linear journey that begins with them waking up in the morning and announcing to the world that they want BOTOX. In fact, new research has shown that the journey probably began ten years ago. Like a fine single malt, the desire to have treatment matures over time, and today that journey has led the client to your door.

But congratulations! You have done a fantastic job, your quality has shone through, and that is why they are choosing to have their treatment with you.

Sounds better than "because you're the cheapest", doesn't it? There is one absolute truth that I will come back to again and again, and that is that cost is not the consumer's primary motive in buying anything. The real drivers when they're choosing to have an aesthetic procedure are:

- Trust – will this person disfigure me?

- Fear – will it hurt?

- Value – am I getting any added value?

These are all considerations, and we cannot create customers or clients until we have effectively addressed them. The core factor in them is emotionality. People buy based on emotion, then use logic to justify it. If we know that our customers purchase this way, then we need to bring it into our process and plan to create business partners right from the beginning.

- Acquisition (How we attract a new lead)

- Activation (Turning them into a client)

- Consultation (Delivering our solution)

- Retention (Following up)

CONSIDERER VS CUSTOMER VS PATIENT

These are the key groups. They are all different and have different goals, so it's interesting to note that one of the big things I see happening in clinics is that everyone is treated the same. Everyone is treated as if they're patients, which is completely the wrong thing to do. One example of this is using medical terminology on your website. Your web presence is consumer focused, right? A Considerer is in acquisition mode, not ready to be treated, and yet they are bombarded with information about heavy chains, light chains, accessory proteins, acetylcholine or the neuromuscular junction.

Considerers are looking for information on outcome. It's as simple as that. They're looking in Activation mode for a reason – they're considering and they don't know where to go, so they are consuming relevant information, and "relevant" is the key.

Let's look at this in context.

You wake up one fine Sunday morning and log on to Facebook to see that someone's taken a photograph of you not looking your best at the barbecue last night. As we are all our own worst critics, you say, "Ugh! Look at the state of that. I really need to do something about this."

Now you're into the mindset of a Considerer of anti-aging products. You're not actually ready to have anti-aging products because you don't know enough about them, but you're open to absorbing information and ready to listen. When you hear about treatments, you tune in. So a great question now is, "What information do practitioners need to provide to tune a Considerer in?"

Well, I can tell you for nothing that overly technical jargon ain't it. One way to find out what information to provide is to look at your avatar. Sometimes we can be a little too broad on our types of patient or customer, and I've made this mistake in the past with some of my products. To get the clarity I needed, I had to define my target customer as an "overwhelmed aesthetic business owner".

Your avatar needs to be specific in order to hit the right emotional cues. Use your avatar research to answer the following questions:

- What does the client want to achieve from the information they are looking for?

- What information are you going to provide?

- Where are you going to put it?

- Where are they going to read it?

What is the purpose of all this? The purpose is to set out your value proposition and clearly articulate what it is that you actually sell. The only way you're going to be able to answer this is to change your own mindset and stand in the shoes of the avatar you want to attract.

THE ACQUISITION PATHWAY

The consumer journey begins with a simple desire – an emotional response to an event that triggers a reaction. The desire to fix a problem will hopefully connect the Considerer with your brand vision and promises, and it's here that the work on the customer avatar pays off. Imagine if you had spent your time creating a brand targeting the millennial market, only it actually appeals to GenX.

The Considerer's second step is "Search". Historically, Google would have been the go-to mechanism to search out a solution, but increasingly Facebook and word of mouth are becoming important. Ideally you would cover all of your bases, but if you are on a budget, I would go for the following as a template for a good social media effort. One single well-structured Facebook Live could give you:

- Four 500-word blogs per month

- One 500-word e-shot per month

- Twenty Facebook posts per month.

This should give you a decent amount of coverage across multiple platforms. It's a fair amount of work, but remember you can outsource this to someone. From the moment they consider aesthetic treatment to the time they're showing off the results of your work to their friends, your clients are going through this journey.

Acquisition. They are looking for information to make a decision on which service provider to choose.

Activation. The Considerer has decided to go ahead with a treatment and is looking for reassurance they will get good value for money.

Consultation. Your Patient is looking for their expectations to be met and for a successful outcome.

Retention. Your Customer has had their treatment and is looking for reasons to become loyal to you as their service provider. They now return to the Acquisition stage and look for information on future treatments. They also want to share their experience with their peers and friends.

To make a journey great, transition your clients consciously through every stage. Remember the Apple Store? Think about all the ways in which you can add value to this process.

For example, what about this experience?

"Good morning, I'm Stacie, here for my 10am appointment."

"OK, great – take this form, have a seat in our waiting area and fill it out. You'll be called when we're ready for you."

There is nothing wrong with this, if you are buying cheese.

Some businesses are very welcoming, but let's go above and beyond and apply some real new level thinking. The door is opened by someone who knows Stacie's name, because when the client booked, that was recorded.

"Good morning, you must be Stacie." (Everyone likes to hear their own name.) "Welcome to The Clinic. My name is Amy, and I'll be looking after you. We need to take some details from you, so please come with me and we'll go through it."

Small changes = big difference.

Your front of house has now taken control of the consultation and is leading the client through the registration process. There are two key objectives to identify here:

- Are we suitable for each other?

- Can your client get a positive outcome?

These are important questions, and ones that aren't asked often enough. I have talked about the different types of business relationships that we all experience, the ultimate goal being to have lots of business partners and avoid the bears at all costs.

So the questions to ask yourself during the consultation are essentially, "Will I be able to turn this customer into a business partner, or have I got myself a master/slave?

Are there any underlying psychological issues I should be aware of?" Stacie comes to see you for a lip treatment, and her partner comes along to provide support. He insists on sitting in on the consultation to provide suggestions on the treatment outcome as he is paying for the treatment.

Six months later, you receive a letter from a solicitor, claiming that Stacie didn't want treatment. She was coerced into it by her partner, and as a professional, you should not have treated her. Now clearly in your mind the client consented to being treated, but unbeknown to you, her relationship was abusive and she was seeking an escape. Now, six months later she has freed herself from this horrible situation but is extremely angry and her lip treatment is a constant visual reminder of her fragile emotional state.

She is seeking recourse and someone to blame, and you are first on the list. Was what you did ethical? This may be an extreme example, but obviously the ideal time to have dealt with it would have been at the beginning. Imagine if you had performed a health check, and in the process asked her partner to leave the room. Then you could have asked the client some questions around why she wanted this treatment and uncovered that she was not 100% committed to it. You would have discovered a bear, and it would have been wiser not to take her on as one of your goals is to create and nurture business partnerships. You can't work with everyone. Sometimes the best thing to do is acknowledge this and move on rather than engage in a destructive relationship. Once you have established that you can work with a client, you have shared goals. You can then confirm and formalise your relationship with your new client.

CLIENT PATHWAY

A useful way of ensuring that you comply with this kind of structure is to visualise the process from the moment a client walks into your business to when they leave. At all times they should be part of a well-honed process that adds value and creates a compelling client experience. The creation of added value is the responsibility of every single person involved in your business. As a leader, you need to set the standard of excellence and ruthlessly hold your business accountable to that standard. The initial welcome is a very important part of the journey. Whether you are working in a busy clinic, a home studio or you're a mobile practitioner, you only get one chance to make a first impression, so make it count. Many clinics have a similar layout to a GP surgery with a massive desk that the receptionist hides behind. If we think back to the Apple retail experience, all purchases are made with an individual, not a till. So welcome your client with a big smile and open arms. The registration process immediately follows the welcome, and you cannot begin the consent process in the waiting room. I have seen many clinics try to save time by asking the client to complete the registration form and then read and sign a consent form. This is the wrong place to do it – increasingly, businesses are sending consent ahead of the appointment time.

"Look! It's moving. It's alive. It's alive… It's alive, it's moving, it's alive, it's alive, it's alive, it's alive, IT'S ALIVE!"

HENRY FRANKENSTEIN – FRANKENSTEIN (1931)

CREATING NEW OFFERINGS

One tricky thing I get asked is, "How do I know what new treatments to offer?"

I think of this as your Service Suite – your provision of world-class products and services for your adoring public. Creating this is an art as well as a science, and it's a continually moving feast. I'm going to give you an actual real-life example of how we create our products and services to give you a framework to use to assess your own Service Suite. The process began with an idea based on a problem that needed solving. In the case of the AE Programme, I was talking to lots of people interested in either beginning an aesthetic business or looking to inject some renewed enthusiasm and energy into an existing product or service offering. Looking around the market, I noticed that there was limited support and guidance for new businesses. Time to clear the whiteboard, assemble the team and discuss.

At the top, I wrote out the customer problem, in this case: "How do we help a new business get from zero to twenty customers?" Even if you're an established business, you can still grab a pen and write down the biggest issue you're facing right now, because this model works well for every case.

The model puts the definition of a new business vs an established one at 100 clients. If you have fewer than 100 active customers (not a mailing list, but people who have bought from you), your key business goal is to grow. If you have more than 100 active customers, your key business goal is to grow and leverage. Once your business is established, you can look into creating extended offerings and adding new products and treatments. It's difficult to focus on getting new business and leveraging at the same time, especially if you have limited resources, so in that crucial early phase, concentrate on getting new clients.

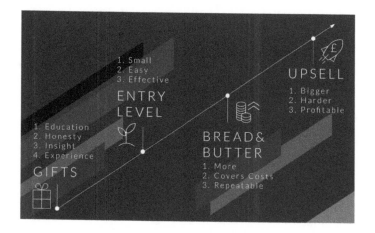

GIFTS

This begins with the customer at the start of their journey, looking ahead. Your goal is to get them to take the first step. You need to know a bit about your customer at this point in order to create a compelling offer for them. There is nothing nefarious about giving something away to gain interest, but it needs to be of actual value and targeted at your avatar – don't give a bald man shampoo. I like to give away knowledge in the form of articles, blogs, scorecards or videos in exchange for an email address. My entry point for a start-up business owner could be encouraging them to read this book, watch a video, come to a talk – something to engage with them and create a conversation. With Aesthetic Entrepreneurs, my team and I looked in depth at what a start-up aesthetic business needs, and we decided that a really useful thing would be to give them a sample of our core products. If the owner joins us, they already have a free business support module on how to create their own Business Scorecard, Product Development Model, and access to the MAETRIX.

In the case of your own gift, what can you offer to get engagement?

What knowledge, wisdom, free blogs or videos can you provide?

Remember, at this stage it's just to get engagement.

ENTRY LEVEL

Once a new prospect has engaged, you need to promote your core product to them. In the case of Medical Aesthetics, this is pretty straightforward – it's injectables. Or is it? I would recommend that you actually create a unique brand offering that is specific to you. Jot down everything that you provide as your core treatments.

BREAD & BUTTER

Now you are in a pretty decent place to create your Key Marketing Assets. These are your fundamental sales and marketing assets – the building blocks that will enable you to maximise your model.

PLAN > BRAND > CONTENT > CAMPAIGN > CHANNEL

This process is designed to uncover the true value of your business and give you a strategic five-stage plan that tailors the perfect message to deliver to your target demographic. Once your clear plan is determined, look at your brand. This is a more involved process than "whacking a logo on it". I've been fortunate to have been collaborating long-term with Russell Turner, a brand developer with over twenty-five years' experience. You've probably seen examples of Russell's work as he is the creative talent behind Hotel Chocolat's brand and the AE logo! Russ specialises in using pack-typing techniques to uncover the hidden value and achieve a brand that connects on an emotional, physical and spiritual level. I spoke to him about the creative process for start-ups:

"Creativity is something that we as human beings have a natural aptitude for. This, however, can be buried beneath the need to excel at so many things when you embark upon a new business venture. I try to encourage business owners to recognise that just because they may not paint or draw, they have a creativity that they can tap into and that they can surprise themselves with. Sometimes all it requires is an open mind."

After the branding stage, it's time to work on your content. At this time, with the help of the whole team, assess your other content tools such as imagery and video, if this is relevant to your campaign. By the time you finish this stage, your microsite and campaign content will be complete. It's all very well having the right content, but if you don't know how to broadcast it correctly then you are fighting a losing battle. Focus, choose the right channels for your content, and devise a plan to help you own those channels. Once you have chosen the right channels, get to work on your campaign. Determine a clear target and objective for the campaign, segment your database accordingly, and then run your campaign throughout the entire management process. Design adverts, landing pages and thank you pages to make the reporting process as accurate as possible.

By the time you finish this process, you will have your lead-generating freebies, your core product offering, your marketing plan, your brand, a website, content and a campaign. Now comes the final part. I recommend that you let the campaign run for at least

---

"In sales, life and business,

the importance of timing

cannot be overestimated."

a month in advance of your launch. Set your launch date for about six weeks' time and promote it now. So how the hell are you going to find the time to implement all that? The truth is, you won't. Some of the knowledge I've shared with you in these pages you won't have the time or skillset to implement yourself, and this is a key point. Outsourcing marketing is one of the most effective moves any business can make. Unless you can afford to have a full-time in-house marketing manager, create and own the marketing plan, but delegate the implementation of it. Remember, there is a difference between delegation and abdication – you delegate the task, not the responsibility. Get the right people in the right place, doing the right things, and you'll get the right result.

UPSELL

In sales, life and business, the importance of timing cannot be overestimated. A fantastic idea that arrives into the market at the wrong time will fail, yet the same product repackaged and rein-troduced a few years later will be a rip-roaring success. The same logic applies to your sales process. Upsell too early and you'll break the bond with your client, potentially destroying your developing relationship. For aesthetic businesses that want to maximise their profit ethically, perfecting a sales journey that upsells without applying pressure is the key to unlocking the potential. The sim-plest way to do this is to have a strict and documented consulta-tion and sales process. Your consultation has two functions – a medical function and a commercial function. Accept this, and it all gets easier.

A well-known plastic surgeon once said to me that in the cosmetic industry, there is a big pot of gold between the client and the healthcare professional which will challenge the professional's ethics. Your goal is for your clients to become business partners, and your business partners benefit from a greater understanding of procedures and more realistic expectations. This leads to higher levels of satisfaction, reduced complaints and ethically increased profitability for your business. In the UK we have an unstable regulatory environment, manifesting itself in confusion and inconsistency. Client belief systems are not challenged at the point of sale, we have exceptionally low levels of differentiation, a growing practitioner base, and poor data capture and record keeping. This is not a recipe for the long-term success of our industry, and it cannot persist.

The consultation is the absolute cornerstone of the process, so why is the goal to make it quick? This is the antithesis of what the speciality needs. Mindsets need to change from the top of the business down to the client.

Here is a process that will add revenue to your bottom line, or anything else you want to promote, and it's the simplest method in the world. I want you to find a good quality sun protection cream. Take that cream and add a markup to the price that you feel is fair, then tell every client you see about the dangers of UVA/UVB radiation. Tell them that this cream is the one you use and it's the best you have come across, and it will protect their investment in themselves if they use it too. Keep in mind, you must have an ethical approach. If you don't use the cream, don't say that you do. See how much of the cream you sell in the first week, the first month. This is true passive income, and a simple upsell technique that will add profit to your business. If you don't believe me, try it out. In this exercise, you have begun to design your pathway and plan the sales and treatment process for your client. Design is important. By not allowing your pathway to drift and meander, you can have focused discussions that maximise your brand and create business partners.

"Show me the money."

ROD TIDWELL – JERRY MAGUIRE (2006)

THE SALES JEDI

Many aesthetic practitioners feel uncomfortable with sales because they believe the myth that a good salesperson can sell snow to an Eskimo. Sales is not about getting one over on people; it's about building trust, developing deeper relationships and gaining a new level of understanding. Sales are the lifeblood of your business, and sales make everything better. I've never forced a sale; it's just not worth it. Why convince someone to have a product they don't need? In order to keep the lifeblood of revenue cascading through your business, you need to create an effective in-clinic sales process. Keep these two things in your mind throughout the rest of the book – the purpose of a consultation is to gain a new level of understanding, and people buy on emotion and justify with logic. If you think of sales as simply positioning a solution to someone who needs it, rather than selling outright, it's easier to reconcile with an altruistic care-giver personality. By having a clear process, you'll achieve two things. Firstly, it will produce a compliant professional journey that satisfies the ethical requirements for a consultation, medical history and record keeping; and secondly, it will satisfy your business's requirement for making money. It is possible to do both. As professionals, most of us already make sales every day of our working lives. Think about how a doctor may explain a diagnosis to someone who has a sporting injury. To begin with, they probably ask them what they have injured. They then think about the solution, how they will fix it, and explain this to the patient in a way they can understand, agreeing on the next steps and proceeding with the treatment. The consultation is exactly the same as a sales process, and like any sales process, you start off with an agenda.

"So, you've come to see about how BOTOX can help you to look a bit younger?" This is a simple closed question designed to set an agenda. Agendas are key in ensuring that you and your client are on the same page and will help to explore and establish what kind of relationship you are going to have. The obvious time to do this is when a new client first registers with you. It is tempting to speed through this part of the client journey, but if you do you will miss a crucial opportunity to build a relationship. I strongly recommend that you sit down with your client, have a discussion and gain a high level of understanding, rather than just hand them a form to fill in. This is the first impression that a new client will have of you. They are looking for value, and you are being evaluated and compared to every buying experience that they have had – you are being compared to lifestyle experiences, not medical, because you are providing an experience.

So this first impression is incredibly important as it will set the tone for your ongoing relationship. Any effort that you invest in this period will pay you back 100 times further on in the journey.

The trick is to have a plan, and the plan is to take every single customer type and have a strategy for them. We need to have business partners; we spend a lot of time with them, and we get a lot of revenue from them. The worst relationship is the bear. We spend a lot of time with them but get very little buy and revenue in return because they're difficult to deal with and take an awful lot of resources to look after.

One of the great benefits of running your own business is you get to choose whom you work with. I don't entertain bears. If I feel that a customer is trying to bully me into doing something that I don't feel is in their best interest, it's my decision to get rid of them as quickly as possible. I can do this by basically refusing to work with them, or by whacking the price up to a ludicrous number. The bear relationship is a complicated one, as it is always emotionally charged. Elon Musk, the CEO of Tesla, publicly identified a bear in relation to a complaint from a potential Tesla customer. This customer vocally called him out on being two hours late for an event and not providing any dinner. Elon took umbrage at this, personally cancelled his order, and has banned him from buying Tesla. That may be an extreme example of a master/slave relationship. Did the customer have a point? Should Elon Musk have apologised and made good in some way? Or did Elon Musk spot a potential nightmare scenario where a vocal, media-savvy customer would be publicly chastising him for every little thing? Business is not a linear process, and sometimes things don't go to plan. It's far better to be working with a supportive customer who understands this and values your products as opposed to someone who screams down the phone at you over any little problem.

I like the idea of being loved and creating products and services that are loved by the people who use them. It's great for the ego and feels wonderful when a customer says, "well done", or even gives you advice on how to improve.

Business Partners

Revenue

Best Friends

Time

Fling

Basic Exchange

Buddies

Bear Ownership

There is one customer group that does this: your business partners, and your business strategy is simple. Make more of them. The strategy required to create business partners from your existing relationships shouldn't be complicated. Here are a few tips on how to turn a couple of other business relationships into business partners to get you started.

THE BEST FRIEND

The simplest way to maximise ATV, or Average Transactional Value, is to put up your prices. However, with best friends this is difficult. They are loyal and love your business, and you have a long history, but you're fed up with not making any money. So the conversation goes a bit like this:

"Hiya, you know you've only been paying £100 for this for some time? Well, now I'm going to charge you £200."

They look hurt, and say, "Hey, but I thought we were friends." They enjoyed feeling special, one of your inner circle. Now you either feel guilty and back down or stick to your guns and the relationship is gone. There is another way you could get revenue from the relationship, and that is by changing your perspective. If you transfer revenue to value, you can have a different conversation. You can assign value to them by asking them to be an advocate or evangelist:

"You've been coming to me for ages, would you mind writing a case study for me?" or "I'm having an open evening. Would you please tell your friends and maybe talk on the night about your experiences?"

In each case, the response will almost certainly be, "Oh yeah, of course. No problem. We're friends." That case study or open evening could be worth thousands in additional revenue through referral, and you can write off the low price you charge your friend as your marketing budget. A simple change can have a huge impact.

THE FLING

With the fling relationship, price doesn't matter so much because there is no loyalty. However, you can create loyalty through upselling. Upselling is a process of adding additional related products to a sale, and it can be extremely lucrative.

A common upsell technique is used in the fast-food industry with the questions "Would you like fries with that?" or "Would you like to go large?"

In the context of aesthetics and beauty, the upsell focuses around a treatment plan that brings long-term benefits and commitment. 'Cause if you like it, then you should have put a ring on it," as Beyonce would say. We spend a huge amount of time with our customers and clients, and they have the right to demand that we maintain our commitment, skills, talents, honesty and integrity. We have the right to work with people who respect us, and by mapping our business relationships and accurately selecting our clients, we can enjoy greater success. Ultimately, it's up to us to create the type of business relationship that we want. During the agenda setting phase, you can really explore this with your new customer. I would recommend that you are able to answer the following questions before you accept them into your business:

- What kind of avatar are they?

- Are they a potential business partner or a potential bear?

- Can you meet their expectations?

Only by spending time engaging and talking with them will you fully understand what they want, identify any potential issues and add value. Remember, by adding value you are creating an experience.

"Make it so."

JEAN-LUC PICARD – STAR TREK: THE NEXT GENERATION,
EPISODE 1 "ENCOUNTER AT FARPOINT" (1987)

FINAL THOUGHTS AND NEXT STEPS

Well, we have reached the end of this part of our journey together. I hope you have found and continue to find this book useful and of value. I have very much enjoyed writing it and sharing some of my story with you. Every single technique and piece of guidance in this book is designed to help you create the best businesses you can, and grow a successful business based on sound ethics and core principles. From creating your plan and identifying your customer avatar, to providing a coherent brand that connects on an emotional, physical and spiritual level; from creating high-quality products and services to providing a clear and compelling consultation that educates and informs; from creating content that engages with your potential clients to ethical client selection, these are all opportunities for you to differentiate yourself from your competition. I really wish you the best of success with your business, whatever stage it is at. I appreciate that you have been given a greatdeal to think about in this book, and I want you to get as much value from it as possible. I want you to apply the models we have outlined, always keeping this in mind.

Building anything of note or value takes three times as long and costs four times as much than you EVER imagined. You're in this for the long haul, you'll make horrible mistakes, have brilliant successes and make mistakes again. If I could go back to the guy sat in his car after walking out of Allergan, I'd tell him it would be alright, trust yourself and your talent, you'll be more successful than you think.

Consistency and discipline are the keys to success.

"I'm very proud of the journey my business has been on, and I can honestly say it wouldn't have happened without the Aesthetic Entrepreneurs. I would be doing Botox in my home clinic for a few people here and there, not giving them more value with me, engaging many more clients or growing my business at this rate.

I am so excited to get to this stage. I still worry and wonder, what next? but I know I have the insight and the best support to get to where I want to be." K

The secret to growing a business online is really bloody simple – you MUST get into the habit of turning up for your people.

TURN UP PREPARED

TURN UP UNPREPARED

TURN UP SHOWERED

TURN UP JUST FROM THE GYM

TURN UP IN THE GYM

TURN UP WITH THE FAMILY

TURN UP IN THE CLINIC

TURN UP ON THE SOFA

TURN UP IN THE CAR

TURN UP FOR 30 MINS

TURN UP FOR 5 MINS

TURN UP WITH LOTS TO SAY

TURN UP WITH NOTHING TO SAY

TURN UP HAPPY

TURN UP SAD

TURN UP RAGING

TURN UP CALM

TURN UP WITH A STUPID FACE

TURN UP SERIOUS

TURN UP TO TELL THEM WHY YOU ARE NOT TURNING UP

I've turned up every day for the last 18 months. I've built a high six-figure business (and counting) using social media, and spent about £200 on ads (that did bugger all). It was finding the focus and discipline to consistently market myself and my business to my target clients. It was having the belief that I am world class at what I do. It was learning that people don't want to be sold to on social media. They want to look at pictures of cats doing funny things, other people having better lives than them and to distract from their rubbish day.

It was learning that no one cares about you. Your latest package/offer/deal is the same as everyone else's. They don't care about you. They care about themselves.

It was learning that they won't just hand their money over to you because you have asked them to. Most people work hard to get paid, why should they hand it over to you? It was learning that most people don't even begin to think about this when marketing. It was learning that we don't sell, we solve problems – understand the real challenges people face and be the solution. It was learning that you need to build genuine relationships and actually give a shit about the people you are helping. It was learning to respect your customers, but also respect yourself. They deserve value, but you also deserve to be rewarded.

And finally, you need to remember that I am just a guy, who got it wrong, and then got it right, and will probably get it wrong again. I'm human like you, and anyone can do this. But not everyone will.

So go out there and don't be boring. Be inspiring, be fun, be loud, be noisy, be bold, be challenging.

Be an Aesthetic Entrepreneur.

If you have engaged with the book and used the MAETRIX to support, you will have hopefully learnt a few things to help. If you want to take the next step, all you have to do is complete this scorecard. If you are the right fit for us, one of the AE team will be in contact to book a free coaching call and see how we can help you on your journey.

No strings attached.

"Thank you so much, Richard, you have given me independence, something to be very proud of, skills transferable in many aspects of my life, and I have thoroughly enjoyed the journey and I'm looking forward to the next chapter x" K

The FREE resources we have provided for you include:

- The Business Scorecard to bookmark where you are

- The MAETRIX system

- A workbook to help you design your Product Development Model.

You can also join our amazing and vibrant online community.

Drop me an email at **richard@aesthetic-entrepreneurs.com** and look out for my workshops, events and contributions to the industry press.

https://podcasts.apple.com/gb/podcast/aesthetic-entrepreneurs-get-stuff-done-podcast/id1495236365

No one can actually prepare you for the rollercoaster ride that is entrepreneurship, but I'd like to leave you with a few final tips to help you.

1. Learn to live with feeling a bit sick most of the time

Starting a business, it seems, is not for the faint-hearted. Every day is a roller coaster of extreme highs, extreme lows and adrenaline. I'll be honest, I've learnt to live with it, but I still wake up in the middle of the night sweating.

2. Test

With every new product, I design and then presell it – just a simple mailshot to my customers telling them all about it. If I get a good response, I'll push on with it, but if it falls flat, I know I'm not selling it properly or it's not solving a big enough problem for my customers.

3. Tell everyone what you are doing

There are two schools of thought on protecting yourself and your IP: tell no one or tell everyone. I'm with the latter. Of course, there is always the risk that someone will steal your idea, but isn't it a bigger risk that you will miss useful guidance, advice or feedback just at the right time?

If you are too cautious, maybe you're not as far ahead of the competition as you think. I don't mind telling people about AE, my goals, where I am currently and the next planned update. As the company founder, shout about how great your product is.

4. Move quickly

This is key: you must be quick and nimble. Opportunity presents itself all the time, and I've seen individuals and companies fail to take advantage. This is primarily down to the length of time it takes them to make a decision. Imagine that each decision you make has a 50:50 chance of success, then your intelligence and judgement need to improve the odds. Ask, "Will it drive my business forward?" If the answer is yes, go for it. If no, don't bother.

5. Have a mantra

This helps deal with Tip One.

"One can choose to go back toward safety, or forward toward growth. Growth must be chosen again and again; fear must be overcome again and again."

Abraham Maslow

Remember that everyone you meet is fighting their own battles and trying to get on, so be grateful for your successes, act with integrity, be kind, and be generous. It will be repaid.

Peace Out.

Lightning Source UK Ltd.
Milton Keynes UK
UKHW041331300522
403725UK00002B/32